South Lakeland Cycle Rides

21 Fun Bike Rides in Cumbria,
the Dales and around Appleby

By Dr Jennifer Richards

CICERONE PRESS
MILNTHORPE, CUMBRIA, LA7 7PY
www.cicerone.co.uk

Acknowledgements

I would like to thank Kathryn Ghazali, Phil Allder and Jacqueline Kerr for assisting me in one way or another with the compilation of this book. Also my husband Howard and three daughters Megan, Kate and Bethan for being so patient.

PLEASE NOTE THAT THE AUTHOR'S ROYALTIES – 10% OF THE PRICE OF THIS BOOK – WILL BE DONATED DIRECTLY TO GUIDE DOGS FOR THE BLIND

Front cover photograph by Tim Woodcock

CONTENTS

Routes

'Sheet' refers to the Ordinance Survey Landranger 1:50 000 series

INTRODUCTION

I started cycling as a teenager, going on Youth Hostel tours with friends and family in the Yorkshire Dales, Peak District and Scotland. When our third child was born, and it was no longer logistically possible to go hiking, we turned back to cycling as a means of being out in the country and getting some exercise.

The children enjoyed the experience, at first being pulled along and then progressing onto pedalling. It was essential to stop along the way to keep the day as an enjoyable experience rather than an exercise regime, so we always incorporated places of interest to rest, or the inevitable ice-cream stops!

In December 1998 my husband Howard and I embarked on a cycle ride across Cuba to raise money for Guide Dogs for the Blind, hence the idea of compiling this book based on our own experiences as a family cycling in and around Cumbria.

This cycle guide is aimed at everyone – young, old, fat, thin, fit or otherwise. Cycling is a great activity that you can do at your own pace. To help you find a ride to suit your level of cycling, the rides in this book are graded 'easy' (Rides 1–7), 'moderate' (Rides 8–17) or 'challenging' (Rides 18–21). In addition, at the start of each ride the route distance and a description of the terrain are given.

The rides cover south and north-east Cumbria, but also range into Yorkshire. As far as possible they follow quiet country lanes, so that even in the most popular tourist areas you can still feel that you are getting away from it all. Each ride is accompanied by a detailed map of the route, which is numbered to correspond with points in the text. Most of the rides include places of interest where you can stop off en route and pass numerous pubs and cafés for those important refuelling breaks, should you need them.

Don't feel that you must have a mountain or racing bike or, for that matter, any of the latest fashionable clothes or equipment before you start. The bike that's been gathering dust in the shed will do fine. However, here are a few tips to make a successful day out.

Mechanics

It goes without saying that your bikes should be in good working order – brakes in particular should be working well, especially if you are taking a child on your bike (the extra weight of a child makes quite a big difference to your stopping distance). If your gears are not working properly you will have difficulty getting up a hill or, worse still, become stuck in the wrong gear. It always makes sense to give your bike a quick once over before leaving. Just about every bike shop will provide a service for you if you don't wish to, or can't, do it yourself. If you hire a bike it should already be in good order.

Haynes publish an excellent manual on bike maintenance-called *The Bike Book*. This is well worth purchasing if you wish to do your own servicing and are not familiar with bike mechanics. Carry a selection of tools and spares, including such items as a pump, Allen keys, chain extractor, spare inner tube and tyre levers (in the event of a puncture it is a lot easier to replace the inner tube and then repair the puncture in the comfort of your home), small adjustable spanner and a reversible screwdriver (slot and cross-head).

Cycling with Children

Trailers (designed for carrying one or two children) which attach to the back of your bike are extremely useful bits of equipment and well worth the investment. Most have canopies which can be pulled down over the child in wet or windy conditions leaving them totally protected from the elements. Once the children have outgrown them they can be utilised as luggage transporters.

If you are taking a child with you who is not going to be pedalling remember that they will get colder than you. You may be doing all the sweating but they will be getting all the wind chill. Their feet, legs and hands are likely to cool down the fastest so take gloves and over-trousers with you for the little ones. Young children generally love going out on bike rides typically from six months onwards. They may even fall asleep after a while, which makes for a peaceful day out. As children get older (about three years) you can progress them onto peddling with you – for example, by using a trailer bike (see photograph). These are excellent devices which enable the child to pedal at their own rate or even stop pedalling altogether if they wish. You can cover quite large distances with a child on a trailer bike and it is not as difficult to balance as you may think.

OPTIONS FOR TRANSPORTING CHILDREN

Trailer Bike (below left): these are cheap and easy to install but are generally felt to be unsafe as the child is not strapped in. I would not recommend using one for any journey other than an extremely short trip on a flat road. It would be difficult to ascend any gradient using one.

SAFER CYCLING:

WHAT CYCLISTS CAN DO

1 Follow the Highway Code

Don't: •jump red lights •ride on pavements
(unless they are shared paths) •ride the wrong way
in one-way streets (unless signs say that cyclists
are permitted to do so) •ride across pedestrian crossings

2 Think ahead

•Anticipate drivers' actions •Catch their eye

3 Be visible

•Ride well clear of the kerb •wear bright clothing
•always use lights after dark or in poor day-time visibility

4 Show drivers what you plan to do

Always look and signal before you start, stop or turn. Ride a straight
line past parked cars rather than dodge between them

5 Move over, when it's safe and convenient

Two-abreast is often OK, but try not to hold up other traffic

6 Ride positively and decisively

It helps motorists to understand what you plan to do

Courtesy of the Cyclists' Touring Club

Once a child is on their own bike, you should always have them riding in front of you, rather than to the rear, for reasons of road safety.

Distance and Speed

The rides in this book are designed for anyone to be able to complete. No time estimates are given since everyone will cycle at varying speeds. As a guide a fit club cyclist will average 16mph, a touring cyclist 10mph and a child 5mph. However, we have often taken all day to do a ride 20 miles long with picnic stops and detours for places of interest. The time taken is also greatly influenced by terrain. Some of the shorter rides can be more physically demanding than the longer ones. Do remember not to push yourself too hard and put you and your family off cycling for life. Each ride should be a fun day out!

Clothes and Comfort

Try to ensure that the bike fits you. After all you wouldn't go for a run in the wrong size shoes. The fit of your bike can make a vast difference to your enjoyment. The saddle height should be positioned so that when the pedal is fully extended your knee is still slightly bent. The distance between the front of the saddle and the handlebars should be equal to the length of your forearm. This is often too long for a female, resulting in her having to lean too far forward to reach the handlebars. In this case either change the handlebars, move the seat forward, or consider a different bike. Try to make sure that children's bikes also fit correctly. It is good practice to make sure children are sitting fairly upright, thus ensuring that they are looking at the road ahead rather than the tarmac.

A layer of waterproofs and several layers of thin clothes are the key to maintaining a comfortable temperature rather than having one thicker garment. Try to cycle in loose clothes and avoid tight, non-stretch materials. Make sure that the base of your back is covered when you lean forward or you will get either cold or sunburnt.

A plastic bag over your socks works wonders for keeping your feet dry and warm. Bright tops and reflective bibs are great for keeping the cars at bay. It gives them no excuse for saying 'I didn't see you'.

KEY TO MAPS

 PARKING PLACE

 DIRECTION OF START

 POINT ON ROUTE

 SINGLE CARRIAGEWAY

 DUAL CARRIAGEWAY

 TRACK

 RAILWAY

 LEVEL CROSSING

 GATE ACROSS ROAD

 CATTLE GRID

 BRIDGE

 RIVER

 STEEP CLIMB
chevron points downhill

 GENTLE CLIMB
chevron points downhill

 MEALS & DRINKS

 SNACKS & DRINKS

 VIEWPOINT

 PICNIC AREA

 CHURCH

 ESCARPMENT

 WOODS – deciduous

 WOODS – evergreen

 WATERFALL

 TELEPHONE

CYCLE SHOPS

Location	Name	Telephone
Appleby	Eden Bikes	0176 53533
Ambleside	Biketreks	015394 31245
Ambleside	Ghyllside Cycles	015394 33592
Carnforth	The Cycle Centre	01524 732089
Cleator Moor	Ainfield Cycle Centre	01946 812427
Kendal	Askews Cycles	01539 728057
Kendal	Brucies Bike Shop	01539 727230
Lowick Bridge	South Lakeland Mountain Bike Sales	01229 885210
Morecambe	Bike King	01524 833644
Morecambe	Chain Reaction Cycles	01524 833767
Morecambe	Smalley's	01524 412446
Penrith	Arragons Cycle Centre	01768 890344
Penrith	Harper Cycles	01768 864475
Staveley	Millennium Cycles	01539 821167
Staveley	M&P Cycles	01539 821443
Ulverston	Gill Cycles	01229 581116
Ulverston	Northwest Cycle Sport	01229 584417
Ulverston	Polkinghorn's	01229 582765

CYCLE HIRE (Many of these will drop-off and collect at *your* location)

Location	Name	Telephone
Ambleside	Biketreks	015394 31245
Ambleside	Ghyllside Cycles	015394 33592
Bowness	Blazing Saddles	0800 7314961
Carnforth	Lakeland Cycles	01524 735465
Cleator Moor	Ainfield Cycle Centre	01946 812427
Kendal	Askews Cycles	01539 728057
Lowick Bridge	South Lakeland Bike Sales & Hire	01229 885210
Orton	Orton Post Office	015396 24225
Satterthwaite	Grizedale Mountain	01229 860369
Staveley	Puddle Jumper Mountain Bike Hire	01539 821611

Staveley	M&P Cycles	01539 821167
Ulverston	Gill Cycles	01229 581116
Windermere	Country Lanes Cycle Centre	
		015394 44544

OTHER USEFUL TELEPHONE NUMBERS
Tourist Information Centres

Location	*Telephone*
Ambleside	015394 32582
Appleby	017683 51177
Fell Foot Country Park	015395 31273
Grange over Sands	015395 34026
Ingleton	01524 241049
Kendal	01539 725758
Kirkby Lonsdale	01524 271437
Windermere	015394 46499

Lake District National Park Information Centres

Location	*Telephone*
Ambleside	015394 32729
Bowness Bay	015394 42895
Coniston	015394 41533
Grasmere	015394 35245
Hawkshead	015394 36525

Other information

Name	*Telephone*
Weather in the Lake District (next day)	017687 75757
What's on in Cumbria	015394 46363
7 day forecast for Cumbria	0891 500419
C.T.C. (Cyclists' Touring Club)	01483 417217
Sustrans	0117 9290888

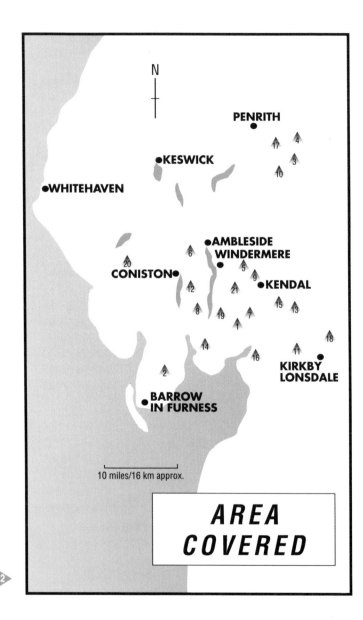

N

PENRITH

17 4

KESWICK

3

10

WHITEHAVEN

AMBLESIDE
WINDERMERE

6

20 5

CONISTON

9

12 21 KENDAL

8 15 13

19 7

14

18

16

KIRKBY
LONSDALE

2

BARROW
IN FURNESS

10 miles/16 km approx.

AREA COVERED

BOWLAND BRIDGE and the RIVER WINSTER

TOTAL DISTANCE – 11 miles/18.6 km
TERRAIN   – Easy, mostly flat

This is a picturesque circular route suitable for children of all ages. There are two very short climbs and the route is very light on traffic, particularly on the return journey.

The Hare & Hounds pub at Bowland Bridge is welcoming to children, providing high chairs and a good range of children's meals. It also provides excellent meals for the adults to enjoy and an outdoor play area for the little ones.

This trip can be combined with a visit to Grange over Sands to feed the ducks and visit the park and promenade or the numerous teashops. You could also take the children for a swim at the Netherwood Hotel, Grange, while you use the steam room, but you will need to pre-book this with the hotel.

Starting point
From the A590 take the road into Lindale. At the mini round-about in the centre of Lindale turn right (from Kendal) or left (from Barrow) down a minor road which is not signposted (next to the Lindale Inn), although there is a signpost as you approach the roundabout – 'Cartmel Fell'. Bear right at the next T-junction to go under the dual carriageway and carry straight on for approximately 2 miles until you reach a cross-roads where parking can be found on the verge.

The ride

⮞ Begin by riding along the road signposted 'Cartmel Fell' from the crossroads.

• After approximately 1½ miles, you pass a furniture maker on the left – worth a look at if he's open.

⮞ Ignore a turning to your left signposted 'High Newton' and continue for a further 1¾ miles, and then take a right turn at the T-junction signposted 'Kendal'.

•The road then descends to Cowmire Hall and a T-junction. Look out for a public footpath sign on the right by a wood. This is a good place to stop for a picnic if you wish.

³▶ At the T-junction, turn left (signposted 'Bowland Bridge and Bowness') down a short hill.

⁴▶ Take the right turn a little further along the road.

•Continue along this undulating road until you reach a T-junction.

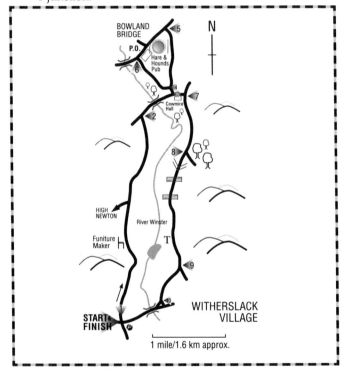

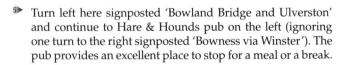

⁵▶ Turn left here signposted 'Bowland Bridge and Ulverston' and continue to Hare & Hounds pub on the left (ignoring one turn to the right signposted 'Bowness via Winster'). The pub provides an excellent place to stop for a meal or a break.

The friendly post office opposite has a tea-room serving light snacks and is well worth a visit.

⑥ After a respite, turn left immediately after the pub (sign-posted 'Witherslack and Grange') and continue straight back to Cowmire Hall.

⑦ Continue past the farm until you reach a junction signposted 'Witherslack' and turn right.

⑧ After a short climb, turn right at the next T-junction (no signpost).
  •Go immediately down a steep hill until you reach a gate across the road. Continue straight through the gate, and also through the next gate, and continue past Strickland Hill Farm and a telephone box on your right.

⑨ Bear right at the next T-junction (no signpost).

⑩ Continue on to a T-junction where you turn right (no sign-post for the right turn).
  •Continue back to your vehicle looking out for plants and flowers for sale at a house on your left.

 **FINISH**

START

RIDE 2

LINDAL to GLEASTON WATER MILL
TOTAL DISTANCE – 10 miles/16 km
TERRAIN – Easy

This route begins at Colony Gift Corporation, Lindal, a factory manufacturing candles and accessories. There is an extensive shop with lots of novel gifts to buy and a seconds selection. Toilets are situated in the shop and there is a café with picnic tables adjacent. This provides a good place to investigate at the end of the ride if you have time to browse and enjoy a rest with refreshments.

The ride passes through rolling countryside and provides relatively easy terrain for a first ride, as nothing is too taxing – even for a beginner. There are several villages to pass through en route, two of which have pubs and one has an upmarket restaurant which also serves morning and afternoon teas.

Mid-way through the ride you pass Gleaston Water Mill. This has a fully working water wheel and a small museum. Tours of the mill can be arranged for groups in advance. At the time of publication, the cost of entry to the museum was £1.50 for adults and 75p for children over four years of age. There is an excellent café next to the mill and space to sit either outside or inside whilst watching the wheel go around. Next to the car-park geese, pigs and highland cattle can also be seen. Adjacent to the mill is a leather shop which will make things to order and has a wide selection of items such as belts and purses.

Starting point
Approach on the A590 Barrow to Ulverston road. When in the village of Lindal in Furness turn following the brown signs for Candle Workshops into London Road. Parking can be found by the side of the road on your right, immediately after turning off the main road, or in the car park of the candle factory if you plan to visit.

Young lamb enjoying the spring sunshine, Cowmire Hall (Ride 1)

Checking a route by Lake Windermere (Photograph by Tim Woodcock)

Winster Valley, looking north from Newton Fell (Ride 1)

Cyclists enjoying morning sunshine, Dufton (Rides 3 and 4)

The ride

1️⃣ Continue along the road to the candle makers crossing a bridge.

• Follow the road as it swings sharply around right past the factory.

2️⃣ Continue along passing Lindal Cote Farm on your right until you reach some crossroads. Go straight across these – signposted 'Stainton'.

3️⃣ Carry along going down a short hill to the next junction where you turn right – there are no signposts.

4️⃣ Take the next left in just over 50 yards – again there is no signpost.

5️⃣ Continue along this undulating road with fields on either side and odd glimpse of the sea until you reach your next junction in the village of Stainton with Adgarley. Turn right here and pass a pub, the Miners Arms, which provides bar meals all day.

6️⃣ Take the left turn directly opposite the pub to pass a farm and a sign for 'Bowes Engineering' on your right.

7️⃣ Carry on until you reach a T-junction where you turn right: no signpost.

• This is a wide road with a gradual climb. Once you reach the brow of the hill you get a good view of the sea. There is then a descent into the village of Gleaston.

8️⃣ Take the first turning on your left as you enter the village, signposted with a brown sign for Gleaston Water Mill and a road sign to 'Ulverston and Urswick'.

9️⃣ Continue past the houses of the village, ignoring three turns into the housing estate, and take a left turn signpost-ed with a brown watermill picture. Follow the brown signs as the road bears around to the right out of the village.

• The watermill can be found in a short distance on your left-hand side. There is a café here, and parking for bikes can be found on your right adjacent to the toilet block.

•Once rested continue on the same road past the mill. You soon pass the ruins of Gleaston Castle on your left immediately adjacent to the road side.

➤ Carry along to reach the village of Scales. As you enter the village you come across a T-junction where you need to turn right – there is no signpost.

➤ Pass a telephone box on your right and take the left turn signposted 'Ulverston'. You immediately pass the village green on your left, where there are some benches to sit on that provide a good picnic place.

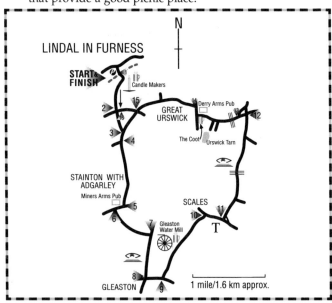

•Climb up the short hill and pass a turning off to your right to Baycliff (the signpost for this cannot be read from this direction).

•Carry along, crossing a cattle grid. There is a short hill immediately after the cattle grid. Once you reach the brow of the hill there are excellent views of Ulverston and the Lakeland fells in the background.

SOUTH LAKELAND CYCLE RIDES

Route 12 Amendment

Due to a recent change in the colour-coding of the cycling routes marked out in the Grizedale Forest, cyclists following route 12 should ignore all references to colour-coded routes.

From the visitor centre, enter the forest as described, and follow signs to Moor Top and High Cross. High Cross is where your route finishes.

The map shows the layout of the forest tracks in more detail, and for 2001 the route you should follow is the GREEN route, as far as High Cross.

Cyclists using this route after 2001 should check with the visitor centre 01229 860373/4/5 or Cicerone Press to be sure to follow a reliable route back to High Cross.

Please note also that the correct telephone number for M & P Cycles in Staveley is: 01539 822884.

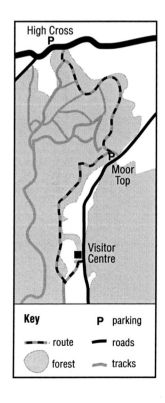

•Continue along downhill past a road off to your right sign-posted 'Sunbrick and Bardsea' until you reach some crossroads.

▶ Turn left at these signposted 'Urswick' (there is sometimes an ice cream van parked here).

▶ Bear left at the next junction to cross another cattle grid.

•Continue downhill to the village of Great Urswick, ignoring a road off to your left as you enter the village and another in the village itself also to the left – neither of these have signposts.

•There is a tarn called Urswick Tarn in the village itself. Access to this can be gained by a public bridleway sign-posted with a usual footpath sign in the centre of the village. This takes you to the water side, although there is no footpath around the tarn.

•At the end of the village you reach a T-junction and a pub on your right called the Derry Arms. The pub does not provide meals, but there is an upmarket restaurant on your left called The Coot which has an excellent reputation and serves morning and afternoon teas.

▶ Turn right here and continue for a short distance, taking the first road off to your left. This is a small road with no sign-post.

•Carry along this road past Causey Wood Farm and house on your left and follow the road as it bears left past some houses.

▶ Ignore one small road off to your right and continue on up a short incline to reach some crossroads. Turn right here signposted 'Lindal and Dalton'.

▶ Continue along soon reaching the next crossroads, where you turn right signposted 'Lindal'. You will recognise this as the road you set off on. Carry along and the candle makers can be found on your right just before reaching your vehicle – don't spend too much!

FINISH

DUFTON FELL near APPLEBY

TOTAL DISTANCE – 11 miles/18.6 km
TERRAIN   – Fairly easy

This route is best done when visibility is good, as you get close to the base of Dufton Fell, with views of the mountains to one side and the plain of the Eden District to the other. Dufton is a classical Dales village with a green in its centre, a post office which sells tea, coffee, and ice creams for the children, and a pub. The Stag Inn has a beer garden and welcomes children.

This is a fairly easy ride with only one very gradual assent out of the Eden valley. The quiet lanes meander close to the base of Pennine peaks making for a relaxing trip.

This cycle ride can be combined with a visit to Appleby Castle. The Castle has 25 acres of parkland, brass rubbing, falconry displays, a medieval activity centre, children's animal garden, deer park, rare breeds and a tea shop. It is well worth a visit.

Starting point
Travel through the centre of Appleby on the B6542, the main street, and head for the A66 Brough, taking the left turn just before reaching the brow of the hill, signposted 'Hilton and Merton'. Go under the railway bridge and immediately fork left up Garbridge Lane. At the top of the lane turn left, signposted 'Brampton and Long Marton', and go under the A66. Parking can be found in approximately 100 yards just on the other side of the bridge on a wide grass verge (see map for details).

The ride

- Start by heading back the way you came, under the bridge for the dual carriageway.

  - Ignore the turning right immediately after the bridge and carry straight on, signposted 'Flakebridge, Hilton and Murton'.

2 Instead of turning right down Garbridge Lane, carry along the side of the A66, signposted 'Flakebridge, Hilton and Murton'.

3 Continue until you reach a T-junction and then turn left under the bridge signposted 'Flakebridge, Hilton and Murton' again.

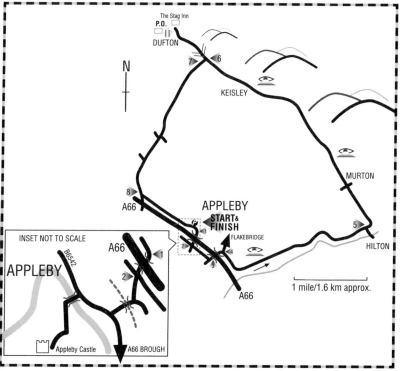

4 Follow the road as it swings around to the right alongside the dual carriageway (ignore the left turn to Flakebridge).

• The road soon veers away from the A66 to follow a small river up to the village of Hilton. You pass Appleby golf course on your right and climb very gradually up with views of the hills.

⁵▶ Once near Hilton carry straight on and do not turn right in to Hilton itself. The road turns sharply left to Murton. This is an undulating road that runs along the base of the fells. You follow the road through Murton and Keisley, following signs for Dufton until you reach the T-junction.

⁶▶ Turn right here, signposted 'Dufton and Knock', climbing up a short hill to reach the village of Dufton. An excellent place to stop for a break and take advantage of the village post office or pub, the Stag Inn. The Stag Inn is a popular watering hole with a beer garden and welcomes children. The village post office also serves tea, coffee and ice cream. They are both found at the far end of the village, next to the water fountain.

  •Once rested it is mostly a downhill ride back to the parking spot. Leave Dufton the way you came in.

⁷▶ Carry straight on, signposted 'Appleby', at the junction you came in on, and after a few ups and downs enjoy a descent past two roads to the right, signposted 'Brampton, L. Marton, Knock and Milburn'.

⁸▶ Just before you reach the dual carriageway turn left sign-posted 'Hilton and Murton'. Stay on this road with the dual carriageway on your right until you reach your parking spot.

FINISH

This is a good route to do as an introduction to cycling. The route is mostly flat or downhill, except for the last pull back up to Dufton itself, which can be taken at a nice slow and steady pace. There are lovely views to be had of both Dufton and the Eden valley plains. The Pennine Way passes through the village of Dufton, so there are always plenty of walkers to be found.

In the village itself there is an excellent pub, the Stag Inn, which provides meals and has a beer garden. Opposite the pub is the village post office which also provides teas and coffee and ice cream (if you are lucky enough to have warm weather).

This route is also a good one to combine with a visit to nearby Appleby Castle, as the cycle ride does not take long.

Starting point
Start in Dufton, parking on the grass verge by the pub, post office and youth hostel.

The ride

▷ Head out of Dufton with the pub the Stag Inn on your right. Go down the hill and continue straight on at the next junction signposted 'Knock and Millburn'. This road forms part of the Cumbria Cycle Way.

• Carry on past St Cuthbert's church. This is a small church in the middle of the field.

• Continue along into Knock with the lovely views of the fells to your right.

② Go through the village of Knock, ignoring a sign to 'Long Marton and Appleby' to your left, and continue on, following signs to 'Silverband and Millburn'.

• Ignore a road off to your right to Knock Christian Centre and carry straight on past a caravan site and a garage on your left. The plains of Eden valley stretch out to the left.

3️⃣ Ignore a road going off to your right which goes to some holiday cottages, and carry on as the road bears around to the left.

4️⃣ Go past Slakes Farm and follow the road as it sharply bends around to the left.

5️⃣ Once you reach the T-junction, turn left signposted 'Long Marton and Appleby'.

•Ignore a road off to your right signposted 'Kirkby Thore'. Continue along the straight road, ignoring a sign to your left signposted 'Knock', and follow signs to 'Long Marton and Appleby'.

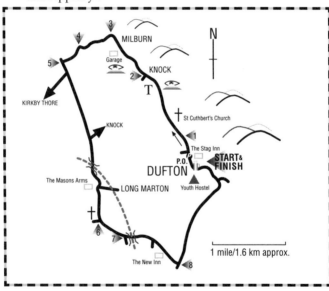

•Follow the road as it winds through the village of Long Marton and go under the railway bridge. The pub the Masons Arms can be found on your right next to a dead-end turning on the right. This pub provides bar meals.

⑥ Continue along through the village past a turning off to your left which has no signpost, following the signs to 'Brampton and Appleby'. Once out of the village, pass a church and road on the right. Continue straight on at this junction, signposted 'Brampton, Appleby and New Inn'.

⑦ Turn left at the next T-junction, signposted 'Brampton'. Go under the railway bridge. As you enter Brampton, ignore a small road going off to the left which is not signposted.

•Carry straight on into the village, passing a telephone box on your left. The pub the New Inn can be found on your right. This provides bar meals and has a beer garden.

•Continue straight on out of the village until you reach a T-junction.

⑧ Turn left here, signposted 'Dufton'. The road at first descends, and then suddenly climbs uphill.

•Go past a road off to your right and carry straight on, signposted 'Dufton and Knock'.

•Once you enter the village of Dufton, carry on straight back to your vehicle for a well-earned rest.

 **FINISH**

TOTAL DISTANCE – 8.6 miles/14.3 km
TERRAIN – Easy

Staveley is an excellent base to use for a circular route. M&P Cycles and Millennium Cycles are cycle shops based here which hire bikes out (see Introduction for telephone numbers).

The village of Staveley has a large playground in which children can unwind after the ride – or before if you need them to burn off a bit of energy beforehand!

The ride covers undulating terrain and passes through quiet back lanes. There are no strenuous climbs involved and, being relatively low on traffic, it is a good route to take children on.

There are several cafés in the village –one in particular, Wilf's (close to M&P Cycles), welcomes cyclists.

The village has several pubs – we have found the Eagle & Child just opposite the playground serves good meals and welcomes children.

Starting point
If approaching from Kendal on the A591, turn right at the first sign to Staveley and continue over the level crossing. Carry on into the village and turn left up the side street immediately after the Eagle & Child pub and before the bridge. You should be able to find space along here to park. If approaching from Windermere, take the first sign left to Staveley. Continue straight on through the village and turn right up the side street immediately after going over the bridge and before the Eagle& Child.

The ride

⬧ Continue up the side street until you pass the pub the Railway Hotel on your left and reach a T-junction.

⬧ Turn left to go under the railway bridge and continue straight up the hill over the main Windermere–Kendal road. This road soon opens out into countryside and you can enjoy the ride to Crook on an undulating road.

3▸ Once you reach the T-junction turn left, signposted 'Kendal'.

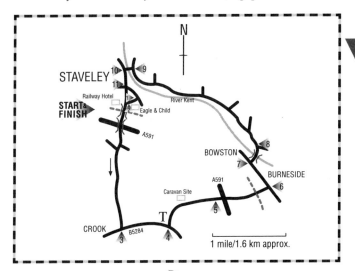

4▸ Pull up a slight hill then descend, taking the first road on your left, signposted 'Burneside'.
•Go straight down this road past the telephone box and caravan site until you reach the dual carriageway.

5▸ Take great care and go straight across the busy road to the road opposite, signposted 'Burneside'.
•Enjoy a long descent before reaching a T-junction just after traversing the level crossing.

6▸ Turn left (no signpost) and go along this road for approximately half a mile.

7▸ Look out for the first turning on your right as you enter Bowston – no signpost and a small road.

8▸ Go down here across the river and bear left at the next T-junction, signposted 'Staveley'.

•Continue straight on, ignoring all roads off to the right, until the road swings around to the left over the river.

9▶ Cross the river.

10▶ Turn left again immediately after crossing the river to take you back to the centre of Staveley.

11▶ Once in the centre, turn left through the village until you pass the playground on your left. Take the side road on your right to return to your car.

FINISH

START RIDE 6 BRATHAY to HAWKSHEAD

TOTAL DISTANCE – 8.7 miles/14.5 km
TERRAIN – Fairly easy

RIDE
6

This is a relaxing ride from the outskirts of Ambleside to Hawkshead along picturesque lanes. The starting point is a lay-by next to the river Brathay which is frequently used by canoeists to paddle down into Lake Windermere. It passes two very popular pubs on the route, the Drunken Duck Inn and the Out Gate, which both provide a good selection of food.

Hawkshead itself is a busy tourist destination with an abundance of places in which to refuel.

There are lots of information booklets available from the tourist information centre about the village and its history, especially on Beatrix Potter.

You return to your car using small roads which pass through the tranquil back lanes of this busy tourist area.

Starting point
From Ambleside head out on the Coniston road and take a left turn on to the B5286, signposted to Hawkshead, approximately ¾ mile outside Ambleside. Almost immediately go over a bridge and park in the lay-by on your right-hand side after the bridge. From Hawkshead follow the road to Ambleside (B5286) to find the lay-by on your left-hand side just before crossing the bridge.

The ride

▷ Take the road off to your right next to the lay-by signposted 'Skelwith Fold'. Go along the road for a short distance with the river Brathay on your right-hand side before pulling away from the river, climbing steadily with woods on either side.

▷ Continue on until you reach a T-junction in the village of Skelwith Fold. Turn left here, signposted Hawkshead, and

29

climb up a short steep hill. You may have to walk up this one!

③ Go past Holmeshead Farm on your left-hand side and carry along to the next junction, in the form of a triangle, with roads off to your right. Continue straight on here – there are no signposts.

④ Carry along until you reach a crossroads, with the Drunken Duck Inn on your right. This is a popular pub providing bar meals. Go straight across the crossroads here – there are no signposts.

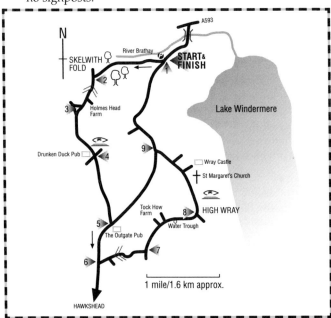

⑤ Carry along this peaceful country lane with easy cycling until you reach a T-junction. Another popular pub, The Out Gate, which stocks real ales and provides bar meals, is situated directly opposite. Turn right at this junction, signposted 'Hawkshead'.

⑥ Pass one road off to your right near a camping ground and

take the next left-hand turn. Watch out for this as it is a small lane and is easy to miss with no signposts. (If you wish to visit Hawkshead carry straight on for approximately ⅓ mile to get to the centre of the village. Don't forget to make a mental note of where the turning is for your return journey.)

You pass a small road off to your right, which is unsuitable for motors, and climb gradually, passing through some farm buildings until you reach a T-junction. Turn left here – there are no signposts.

RIDE 6

•Go past a small road off to your left leading down to Tock How Farm and past another small road off to your left soon after. Opposite this second road there is a water trough at the side of the road dating back to 1891.

Carry on until you reach the village of High Wray, where you pass a road off to your right which leads to the ferry (about 4 miles). Go straight on here, signposted 'Wray Castle and Ambleside'.

•Just after exiting the village you get good views across Lake Windermere to your right. Carry along, passing St Margaret's church and Wray Castle and College on your right-hand side in Low Wray.

Go past a small road off to your right-hand side leading to Low Wray campsite and carry on to reach a T-junction with the B5286. Turn right here, signposted 'Ambleside'.

•Ignore one road off to your left and carry straight on, signposted 'Ambleside', to join your car again.

FINISH

START

RIDE 7 LEVENS to CROSTHWAITE

TOTAL DISTANCE – 13.7 miles/22.8 km
TERRAIN – Easy to moderate

This is a pleasant trip which starts by going along the Lord's Plain – a flat area of the Lyth valley – before gaining height to the village of Crosthwaite, where you can find a village inn and children's playground. The reward for the brief climb is a majestic view of the extensive plain bordered by surrounding hills.

There is an excellent playground stop for those with younger children and the inevitable pub stop for the adults, before returning to Levens via Brigsteer Park – an area of woodland owned by the National Trust. This trip can also be combined with a visit to Sizergh Castle and its impressive gardens. This castle, which dates back to Elizabethan times, has restricted seasonal opening times – so check before you set off.

Starting point
The start of the ride is in Levens village itself. The village has quite a complex road system. But parking can be found adjacent to St John's church (not the Methodist church) on Church Road in the centre of the village. You may need to ask locals directions to the church once in Levens.

The ride

1. Start by heading down the road, with the church on your right, to a T-junction. Turn right here (no signpost).

2. Go past the Hare & Hounds pub on your right and then turn immediately left (there is a brown Cumbria Cycle Way sign).

3. Continue along for a short distance before taking the first left turn to go across the small bridge (no signpost).

4. Continue along over another small bridge before taking the first turning on your right (no signpost). This road takes you across the centre of the Lord's Plain.

32

Cyclists in Grizedale Forest (Ride 12)

Coniston Water, village and 'Old Man' from east shore (Ride 12)

Cartmel Village square (Ride 14)

Holker Hall and gardens (Ride 14)

•Continue along, ignoring one road off to your right, and follow the road as it bears right around a sharp corner and over another small bridge.

•The road bends around to the left again, before climbing steeply uphill past some farm buildings to reach the next T-junction.

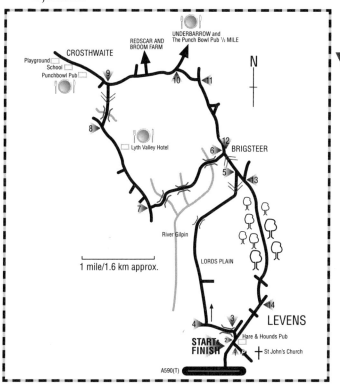

5▶ Turn left here (no signpost) down a steep hill through Brigsteer village.

6▶ Turn left at the 'Give Way' and then immediately left, signposted 'Lyth'.

•Carry along this flat road passing over a bridge and past an ostrich farm to your right – an interesting sight for the children.

7▶ When you join the A5074, the main road to Bowness, turn right. Although this is a trunk road, it is not too busy and is wide, so you don't feel too threatened on your bike. Continue straight along passing an inn – the Lyth Valley Restaurant and Bar.

8▶ Once you have passed this inn, watch out for the next turning right which you need to take, signposted 'Crosthwaite and Kendal'.

•Go over the bridge and climb up the hill to the next road junction.

9▶ Turn left at this junction, signposted 'Bowness' (ignoring a small turning left – no signpost immediately before this junction).

•Cycle through Crosthwaite village, passing the church and The Punch Bowl on your left. The Punch Bowl is a well-known restaurant with a reputation for quality, although it is not the place to take young children if you want to be able to relax! If you have younger children, you can continue through Crosthwaite village looking out for the playground on your left just past the school. It is set back from the road next to the bowling green. There is a sand pit with buckets, and so on, provided and a couple of benches to sit on – an excellent picnic stop for children to burn off energy while you conserve yours.

•For the return journey, exit Crosthwaite village by the way you came in.

•Ignore the turning you came in on, and continue straight on to Underbarrow. Pass a road to your left (no signpost).

•Pass another road off to your left, signposted 'Redscar and Broom Farm', before going down hill.

10▶ Take the next right turn, signposted 'Brigsteer, Milnthorpe and Levens' (if you wish to visit the Punch Bowl pub in Underbarrow which provides bar meals, do not take this turn but carry straight on, ignoring roads off to your right and left, for approximately another half a mile).

⯈ Climb gently up to reach the next T-junction. Turn right here, signposted 'Brigsteer and Levens'.
•Continue straight along, ignoring two roads to your left (no signpost).

⯈ Just as you are entering Brigsteer village ignore the first turning off to your right, signposted 'Lyth', and take the next turning immediately again on your right, signposted 'Levens, Milnthorpe and Kendal'.

⯈ Travel back along this road to Brigsteer village (this is the road you came along earlier). Do not take the left or the right turns off through the village but carry straight on until you reach a 'Give Way' sign. Turn right at this give way (no signpost).
•This road takes you through Brigsteer Park, an area of National Trust woodland.
•Continue along this road, going straight through the cross-roads signposted 'Levens and Milnthorpe'.

⯈ At the next T-junction turn right into Levens village itself. Continue straight on through the village, keeping on this road the whole time until you pass the Hare & Hounds pub on your left-hand side.

⯈ Turn left immediately after the pub to get back to the church and your car.

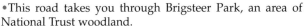

FINISH

START RIDE 8 GRIZEDALE, STOTT PARK and LAKESIDE

TOTAL DISTANCE – 11 miles/18.3 km
TERRAIN – Undulating

This ride starts at a Forestry Commission car park not far from Grizedale visitors' centre, where there is a café, playground and gift shop with an audio visual display.

The main stopping point on the ride is Stott Park Bobbin Mill. This is an English Heritage site consisting of an early 19th century mill. Tours are given around the mill which is open from 10am–6pm daily (April–November). The last tour starts at

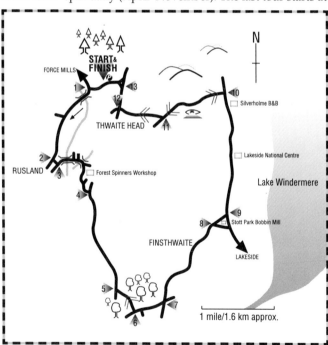

5pm. There is a small gift shop which stocks ice creams, as well as toilets and a museum section (no charge for entry). Every Tuesday and Thursday there is an opportunity to see the steam engine in operation. During April to October there are battle re-enactments, music and drama events held (tel. 0171 973 3434 for event dates).

This ride can also be reached by using the Lakeside Steamers which run from Ambleside and Bowness. The point of entry to the ride is detailed on the map.

By taking a short diversion (about 1¼ miles) you can reach Lakeside itself. Apart from the obvious boat trips to Ambleside and Bowness there is also an aquarium where you can walk through an underwater tunnel and see over 30 displays. The Lakeside to Haverthwaite Steam Railway also leaves from this point and operates from April to November. Needless to say there are plenty of opportunities to obtain drinks, ice creams, and so on here.

Starting point

Start at Blind Lane Forestry Commission car park near Grizedale visitor centre. Head south from Grizedale through the village of Satterthwaite and take the left turn just before entering the village of Force Mills. The car park can is a short distance on your left-hand side and is clearly signposted Blind Lane.

The ride

▶ Turn right at the exit of the car park. Carry along for a short distance into the village of Force Mills, where you turn left at a T-junction signposted 'Rusland, Oxen Park, Colton and Ulverston'.

• Carry along through the village, passing over a bridge and ignoring a small road off to your right.

▶ Continue until you reach a road off to your left, which you take, signposted 'Rusland Cross, Newby Bridge and Haverthwaite'.

▶ Continue for about 50 metres and then turn left again (at the time of publishing there were no signposts at this second junction).

• Carry along, crossing a bridge and passing two roads off to your left–ignore these and carry straight on. Immediately after the second road off to your left you cross a bridge and climb a short hill.

• Pass another very small road to your left, which you ignore.

• The incline soon eases and you continue to pass the Forest Spinners Workshop and another road also on your left. Again, carry straight on, signposted 'Haverthwaite and Newby Bridge'.

You soon reach the village of Rusland Cross, where the road veers sharply around to the left. At the T-junction in the village you turn right, signposted 'Newby Bridge and Haverthwaite'.

The road then descends to the valley floor and you follow the valley along for some distance until you reach a road off to your left signposted 'Finsthwaite and Newby Bridge'. This is the road that you need to take.

This road climbs steeply up for approximately half a mile through woods on either side. When you reach the T-junction turn left – signposted 'Finsthwaite'.

You soon pass a road off to your right, which you ignore, and carry straight on until you reach some crossroads. Turn left at the crossroads signposted 'Newby Bridge, Finsthwaite, Lakeside, Graythwaite and Hawkshead'.

Carry along passing through the village of Finsthwaite itself, ignoring one small road off to your left soon after the village. Continue until you reach the next junction, where you follow the sign for Stott Park Bobbin Mill.

• Carry along, passing the upper car park for the mill, until you reach a T-junction. Turn left here to gain access to the main car park for the mill. As mentioned in the introduction to this ride, it is well worth a visit.

• If you wish to take a small diversion to Lakeside you need to turn right at this junction and continue for approximately 1¼ miles. (This is where the aquarium, steam railway and Lakeside Steamer trips are available.)

After visiting the bobbin mill turn left out of the exit to the car park. You soon pass a small road off to your left, which you ignore and carry straight on.

•Carry along past Lakeside National Centre on your right (an outdoor pursuits centre) and Silverholme bed and breakfast, also on your right.

Once past the bed and breakfast look out for the next turning on your left, which you need to take, signposted 'Rusland and Satterthwaite'.

•This road soon begins to climb quite steeply. Make certain you are in a low gear, as this goes on for some time. Once past a sharp bend with a house on the corner you are nearing the top of the hill.

The road then descends steeply, with good views over Grizedale forest, to reach a fork in the road. Right here – there are no signposts – and continue to descend steeply.

The gradient eases off, and the road then passes through a cluster of houses (Thwaitehead) before reaching some crossroads where you turn right – signposted 'Satterthwaite, Grizedale and Hawkshead'.

Carry along and take the first road off to your left, signposted 'Satterthwaite, Grizedale and Hawkshead'. In approximately 50 yards you pass a road off to your right, which you ignore, and carry straight on until you reach Blind Lane car park on your right.

FINISH

STAVELEY and surrounding fells

TOTAL DISTANCE – 6 miles/10 km
TERRAIN – Two steep climbs

Staveley has two cycle shops, M&P Cycles and Millennium Cycles, which hire bikes out (see Introduction for telephone numbers).

There is a large playground for children to unwind in after the ride – or before if you need them to burn off a bit of energy beforehand!

There are several cafés in the village – and one in particular, called Wilf's, welcomes cyclists.

The village has several pubs – we have found the Eagle & Child just opposite the playground serves good meals and welcomes children.

Although this is a short route, it is, in fact, fairly demanding, since it involves a considerable amount of climbing. The route starts by going along the side of the main Kendal to Windermere road using a cycle path and then passes through

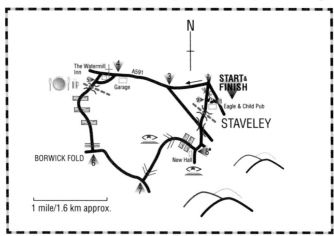

the village of Ings for the first of the climbs, taking you out into quiet unspoilt countryside. You return along part of the Dales Way walking path, passing New Hall before descending back into Staveley.

Starting point
If approaching from Kendal on the A591, turn right at the first sign to Staveley and continue over the level crossing. Carry on into the village and turn left up the side street immediately after the Eagle & Child and before the bridge. You should be able to find space along here to park. If approaching from Windermere, take the first sign left to Staveley. Continue straight on through the village and turn right up the side street immediately after the bridge and before the Eagle & Child.

RIDE
9

The ride

1▶ From your parking spot, go back and join the road through the centre of the village, turning left across the bridge.

2▶ Go straight through the village of Staveley, following signs to Windermere A591.

3▶ Once you've joined the main A591, turn right onto the cycle way on the right-hand side of the road, signposted 'Cumbria Cycle Way'.

4▶ Go along the cycle way for just over a mile and watch out for the first turning off to the left immediately after the BP garage – no signpost.

  •You will need to cross over the carriageway to take this minor road, which passes the church and the Watermill Inn on your right, serving real ales and bar meals.

5▶ Take the next left turn and go through a gate and under the railway bridge signposted with a blue cycle sign for 'Windermere via Borwick Fold'.

  •Continue on the tarmac road into open countryside through three more gates and a long uphill incline. Then descend to the next T-junction immediately after the cattle grid.

⬥ Turn left at this junction – no signpost.

⬥ Continue along this road for just over half a mile, then take the first left after a descent, marked by a small wooden footpath sign 'Dalesway' – easy to miss if you are not careful.

•Go up this steep hill to be rewarded by an equally steep descent and some brilliant views – watch out for the two gates across the road on the descent.

•Go past New Hall on your right down to the T-junction (this road forms part of the Dales Way walk).

⬥ Turn left at this T-junction (no signpost) and continue into Staveley, crossing the main A591 via a bridge and going under the railway bridge.

⬥ To return to your car, take the first right immediately after the railway bridge.

 FINISH

START RIDE 10 ORTON and RUTTER FALLS

TOTAL DISTANCE – 18 miles/30 km
TERRAIN   – Mixed

This route starts from Orton and circles Great Asby Scar, a limestone outcrop, via a short diversion to Rutter Falls where there is an excellent café complete with ford and craft shop. The owners of the café have several varieties of birds which wander around the river and picnic tables. They are welcoming to children, offering a wide range of food and, of course, ice creams – all excellent value.

There is a short stroll to view the waterfall – impressive when in full flow – although that will coincide with rain!

In the village of Orton you will find Kennedy's Fine Chocolates. This is a handmade chocolate factory with ice cream parlour and shop. A good incentive to get up the hill.

The village post office in Orton offers bike hire at very reasonable hourly rates (tel. 015396 24225).

Starting point
If approaching Orton from Tebay, take the first right just as you enter the village, signposted 'Gaisgill, Raisebeck and Kirkby Stephen'. Carry along this road for a short distance past the houses until you reach a lay-by on your left with a seat by a junction.

If approaching Orton from the north, carry on through the village until you reach a sign to your left for 'Gaisgill, Raisebeck and Kirkby Stephen'. Take this road and continue as above.

The ride

➤ Go straight across the crossroads next to the lay-by and continue on to Raisebeck, ignoring a small turning on your left which goes to some farm houses called Scarside.

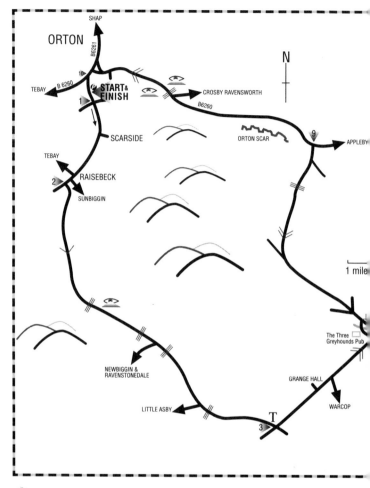

2 Once in Raisebeck, you pass one turning on your right
  signposted 'Tebay' and another immediately on your left
  signposted 'Sunbiggin'. You do not take either of these, but
  carry on to the next fork in the road, where you take the left
  turn, signposted 'Asby and Soulby'.
  • This road climbs gradually before crossing a cattle grid to

reach open moor with beautiful views and a real feeling of the great outdoors.

• Once on the moor you pass some small tarns and another cattle grid and then begin your descent.

• Ignore the first turn to your right, signposted 'Newbiggin and Ravenstonedale', go over a cattle grid, and ignore the next right turn which leads to the tiny village of Little Asby.

3» Continue your descent over yet another cattle grid to some crossroads by a red telephone box, where you turn left, signposted 'Great Asby and Appleby'.

RIDE
10

• Carry on along this undulating road past a turning to your left signposted 'Grange Hall, Asby Grange and Fell Head', and then past a turning to your right signposted 'Warcop', thus descending into the village of Great Asby.

4» Bear right at the T-junction signposted 'Appleby' and continue until you reach a crossroads (ignoring a right turn to Goodlie Hill).

5» Turn right at the crossroads and carry on for nearly 2 miles until you reach a sign for Rutter Falls waterfall on your left.

6» Take this steep road down to the falls and enjoy your ride across the ford and the treats awaiting at the café on the other side.

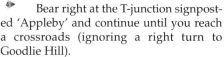

7» After a break return across the ford and turn right at the road junction to head back to Great Asby.

8» When you get back to the crossroads, carry straight across, signposted 'Great Asby', to the centre of the village. The pub the Three Greyhounds can be found in the centre of the village by bearing left across the bridge past the church. If you do not wish to visit the pub, carry straight on. A playground can be found just as you exit the village by a turning off to your left (no signpost).

•Continue straight out of the village, climbing a short hill and following signs for 'Orton'.

•The road levels out and then curves sharply around to the right before climbing quite steeply up and then levelling out at the cattle grid and joining the B6260 Orton to Appleby road.

Once you have reached the 'B' road turn left (no signpost) and head across the open ground, climbing gradually to the top of Orton Scar, and ignoring a sign to your right for 'Crosby Ravensworth' before crossing a cattle grid.

•The road then descends quite steeply, and you can enjoy the ride down into Orton village itself. (There is a café signposted to the right as you enter the village on the Shap road, and a pub, the George Hotel, in the centre of Orton.)

To reach your vehicle again, go straight through the village, following signs for Tebay, and turn left at the edge of the village, signposted 'Raisebeck, Gaisgill and Kirkby Stephen'.

•Carry on to the lay-by.

FINISH

Kirkby Lonsdale is a busy market town with a traditional market square and lots of interesting shops. There are several pubs and tea shops all selling good food. One tea shop, Nutters, on the corner of the market square, is particularly welcoming to children and provides colouring crayons and so on for them.

It is worth a little walk to Ruskin's View from the churchyard. This view over the Lune valley was painted by Turner and became famous countrywide.

Docker Park Farm is a working farm and visitor attraction combined. It is particularly good for hands-on experience with animals. There are regular lamb feeds and tractor-trailer rides, and (when she's up to it) pony rides on weekends and holidays. It is always a good idea to ring them to check the weather, admission prices and seasonal information (tel. 015242 21331).

You can also stop at a toy woodwork shop. This has masses of old-fashioned toys such as rocking horses and spinning wheels. You can watch some of them being made. It's an interesting place to rest, even if you don't intend to buy anything.

Starting point
Park in Kirkby Lonsdale itself. If the market square is full, or it is market day (Thursday), parking can be found by heading out of Kirkby on the road to Old Town, just on the outskirts of town. It is also free to park here, whereas there is a charge for parking in the market square.

The ride

> Once parked in Kirkby Lonsdale, head out of the market square in the centre by going uphill past the post office on your right, and the police station and fire station on your left.

2. Carry on up this road and follow the road around to your right. Then take the first left, signposted 'Kendal'. The signpost may be hidden by some trees.

3. Go along for about 50 yards and then take the first left. This has a little signpost 'Cumbria Cycle Way'. The road goes past Queen Elizabeth School on the right, before joining up with the main A65 trunk road.

4. Go straight across the trunk road, signposted 'Hutton Roof and Burton'. Pass a telephone box on your left.

   •Carry straight on, following the road around as it bears right.

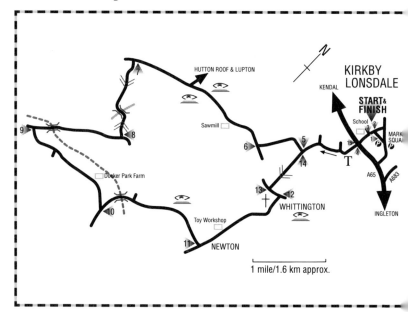

5. Continue along this road, ignoring a turning to your right signposted 'Biggins'. Follow the signs to 'Hutton Roof and Burton'.

   •Ignore another road off to your right signposted 'Kirkby

Barkin Beck, Barbondale – a popular picnic site (Ride 13)

The waterfall and pool, Deepdale (Ride 18)

Cottages and Grizedale Beck, Force Mills (Ride 8)

Rusland Valley, looking west from above Thwaite Head (Ride 8)

Lonsdale' and carry straight on, signposted 'Burton-in-Kendal and Whittington'.

• At the next T-junction follow the road around to the right, signposted 'Hutton Roof and Burton'.

• Continue along this road around some bends going up a gradual incline.

6 The road then flattens out before reaching a T-junction. Turn right at the T-junction, signposted 'Burton and Hutton Roof'.

• Continue along this road as it passes through rolling countryside. Pass Hutton Roof Saw Mill on your left.

• Pass a road going off to the right signposted 'Hutton Roof and Lupton'.

7 Carry straight on going downhill and then gradually uphill. Watch out for the next turn on your left signposted 'Arkholme'. This is the road you want to take. This road has a very steep descent before crossing a narrow bridge and then climbing back up again. The road flattens out before reaching the next T-junction.

8 At the T-junction turn right, signposted 'Borwick'. Follow this road along until it meets the railway line.

9 Cross over the railway bridge and continue to the next T-junction. At this T-junction turn left, signposted 'Arkholme and Whittington'.

• Continue along this road as it rolls up and down past open countryside. Ignore a small turning off to your right which goes to a farm.

• Pass Brown Edge Farm on your left, ignore another small road off to your right, and carry straight on to Docker Park Farm.

10 After resting at the farm, turn left as you come out of the farm car park, and continue on to a T-junction. Turn left at the T-junction, signposted 'Docker and Newton'.

• Pass over the railway bridge and continue straight along this road ignoring the road off to your left. Follow signposts for 'Newton'.

🢂 Continue along this road, which has lovely views of the Barbon Fells. Once at the T-junction turn left, signposted 'Kirkby Lonsdale'.

• After about ¼ mile you pass the toy workshop on your left. This is worth a visit to pick up unusual gift items.

• Continue along the B-road into Whittington, where you will see lovely views of Ingleborough and the Barbon Fells.

🢂 Straight through Whittington, watching out for a left turn which you need to take, signposted 'Hutton Roof'.

🢂 Pass the church on your left, and then immediately after the church take the very small right-hand turn. There are no signposts here, but there is a blue sign saying 'Unsuitable for Heavy Vehicles'. The sign may be hidden by a rhododendron bush.

• This road starts with a steep incline, which does then ease before you reach the next T-junction.

🢂 Turn right at the T-junction, signposted 'Kirkby Lonsdale'. Follow the road around to the right, ignoring a road to your left.

• Continue along back in to Kirkby Lonsdale, ignoring another road off to your left.

🢂 Once back at the T-junction of the A65 go straight across and return into Kirkby Lonsdale the way you came out. It is signposted 'Town Centre'.

 **FINISH**

START

RIDE 12 CONISTON WATER and GRIZEDALE FOREST

TOTAL DISTANCE – 14 miles/23.3 km
TERRAIN   – Mixed

This ride passes Brantwood (the home of John Ruskin, 1872–1900). The house has some exhibitions, video, a bookshop and the Jumping Jenny tea room. Some short walks can be done in the extensive gardens and estates. The house is open from mid-March to mid-November, 10am–5.30pm, and in the winter season Wednesday to Sunday, 11am–4pm.

The route passes two pubs. The Manor House in Oxen Park serves home made lunches and evening meals, and was in the Egon Ronay guide (1993). There is no beer garden but quite a few picnic tables on the patio terrace at the front. The second, the Eagles Head, in Satterthwaite, has a beer garden, serves real ales and provides bar meals.

Grizedale Forest Park has a large visitors' centre which has an audio-visual display, a shop, toilet facilities, an ice cream stand, a small restaurant which serves light meals and an extensive children's play area. There are several walks and cycle routes going from the centre itself, details of which can be found in the shop. There is cycle hire available (see Introduction for details) which also provides trailers and trailer bikes, although it is advisable to phone and book if you require either of these.

Starting point
The starting point is at High Cross Forest Enterprise car park. This is on the B5285 Hawkshead to Coniston road, just opposite the turn for Tarn Hows and Ambleside by Barngates.

The ride

- Come out of the car park and turn left onto the road. The road starts to descend gently before reaching the first road off to your left, which you need to take, signposted 'East of Lake'.

  •This small road drops quite steeply down through some

51

woods before reaching a T-junction in the form of a triangle.

② Turn left here, signposted 'Newby Bridge and East of Lake'. The road climbs up a short hill before starting to undulate.

•Brantwood, the home of John Ruskin between 1872 and 1900, can be found on your left-hand side.

•Once past Brantwood, you continue along with Coniston Water on your right and the woods of Grizedale Forest to your left. You pass the Machell Coppice car park, which is a Forestry Enterprise car park with a 1½ mile walk and

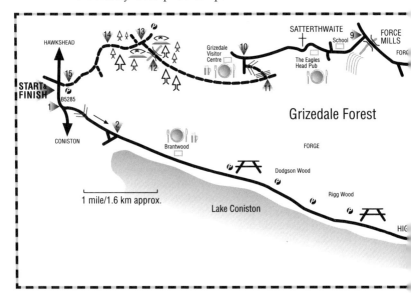

some picnic tables, plus access to the lake shore.

•The road closely follows the edge of the lake with easy cycling. Go past the National Trust car park on your left and continue on to the next National Trust car park also on your left, called Dodgson Wood. This car park also provides access to the lake shore, and any of these car parks provide excellent places to stop for a picnic or a rest.

•The next car park you come across is Rigg Wood, a

Forestry Enterprise car park with picnic table. Continue along as the road becomes lined with rhododendron bushes to pass straight through the village of High Nibthwaite. You have now reached the end of the lake.

3▶ You come to a road going off to your right, signposted 'Wateryeat'. Carry straight on here, signposted 'Newby Bridge'.

4▶ Continue along, passing a road to your left which is a dead end, and carry along the mostly flat road until you reach the next turning off to your left, signposted 'Oxen Park'. Turn left up here. This is a small road which climbs steeply up over the wooded hill you see in front of you. The worst bit of the climb is when you reach the forest and the road bends around sharply right and left. You can always get off and walk here, as you have nearly reached the summit.

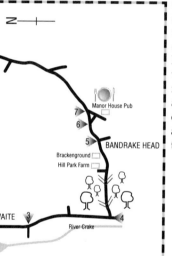

RIDE 12

• Once at the top of the hill you pass a small track off to your left going to a farm called Hill Park.
• Carry along as the road begins to descend fairly steeply through the forest, passing a house called Brackenground on your left.

5▶ You then have a short climb before Bandrake Head. As you enter the village take the first left-hand turn, signposted Rusland, Grizedale, Satterthwaite and Hawkshead'.

• Carry straight along this road, ignoring a small turning off to your left soon after the last T-junction. There is a short descent and climb before reaching the village of Oxen Park.

6▶ At the fork in the village you need to bear left. There are no signposts.

7▶ Very soon after taking this left fork you come across a T-junction, where you need to turn left, signposted 'Rusland, Grizedale and Hawkshead'. There is a pub to the right called the Manor House which serves home-made lunches and evening meals, and was in the Egon Ronay guide (1993).

• Just after exiting the village of Oxen Park, there is a small road off to your left which is unsuitable for motor vehicles. You ignore this and carry straight on.

• Continue to the next signpost, with a road going off to your right signposted 'Bouth', and carry straight on – signposted 'Grizedale'.

8▶ Carry on, ignoring a small road off to your left signposted 'Ickenthwaite'. You soon come across the next T-junctions, where there are two roads off to your right. You need to carry straight on at both of these, signposted 'Grizedale and Hawkshead'.

• Continue along this road, ignoring one small road off to your left with no signpost just before entering the village of Force Forge.

• Pass straight through the village and continue on to cross a small bridge in the village of Force Mills.

9▶ Follow the road around to the left through the village, signposted 'Satterthwaite, Grizedale and Hawkshead'. There is a large sign for Grizedale Forest Park on your right at this corner.

• The waterfalls can be found on your left-hand side and are clearly visible as you climb up the short hill.

• Pass Satterthwaite and Rusland school on your right-hand side and a small road off to the right going to Bowkerstead Farm.

• Carry straight on through the village of Satterthwaite itself, ignoring the small track off to your left before you reach the village. There is a pub in the village on your left called the Eagles Head, which sells real ale and provides bar meals.

• Carry straight on through the village, passing the church

54▶

on your right and ignoring the two roads going off on either side of the church to your right.

•Carry along past Bogle Crag car park on your right-hand side. The road soon reaches Grizedale Visitor Centre. After a rest, continue along by following the blue cycle route, which runs alongside the main building (the one with a clock on top of it) in the Visitor Centre complex. This is signposted 'Moortop and High Cross'.

Follow the road down to cross a small bridge and pass a house on the right-hand side. Take the first left after the house. There is a wooden gate across the track, which you normally have to open.

•There is a green sign with a white cycle on it and a blue arrow, and there is a public bridleway marked. The path is not tarmacked: it is a forest track, but the surfaces are fairly even. The track climbs gradually and then fairly steeply.

RIDE 12

Cross a cattle grid to reach a junction with no signpost at which you need to turn right. There is a further short uphill section before the track flattens off. Keep on the main track, ignoring the walkers' exit to the right.

•There are several points on the track where walking routes converge on the main cycle track. Ignore these and continue along the main track, following the blue cycling arrows.

•After the plateau section, the track begins to rise again fairly steeply. The climb is fairly short before levelling out at the higher elevation. After a short downhill section, the track starts to meander through woods and momentarily comes out of the forest with views to either side.

At a fork in the track, turn right (there is no signpost at the fork) and go over a small bridge crossing a beck. Follow the blue cycling sign just on the other side of the bridge.

•At the top of another moderate climb there is a path off to the left, which you should ignore and carry along the main path.

Shortly after the last turn off, you want a left-hand turn which has a red arrow against it. There is a track veering off to the right which leads to a car park. You do not follow it.

You almost immediately come to another junction, where you turn left.

•At the next fork in the road, veer to the right, following the red arrow and white cycle sign. The track at this point is a very gentle uphill section.

•The track starts to descend quite sharply, with spectacular views of Coniston Water and the surrounding hills, including the Old Man of Coniston.

•There is a left-hand turn off the track, which you should ignore and carry straight on.

•At the next fork in the road, take the right-hand turn where you see a white cycle and a red arrow sign.

•Continue along the main track following the red signs, ignoring the next turn off to the left into the trees.

•After this turn off there is a nice downhill section which goes nearly all the way to the car park.

The road veers sharply to the right with a small track off to the left, which you ignore. The path continues downhill. You can gain quite a bit of speed on the downhill section before the car park, and be warned – there is a barrier across the road just prior to the car park which the unsuspecting cyclist may career into at speed.

FINISH

START RIDE **13** **BARBONDALE to DENT via HOLME OPEN FARM**
TOTAL DISTANCE – 16 miles/26.6 km
TERRAIN – Mixed

This ride starts off in the idyllic village of Barbon and travels up over Barbondale to drop down near the village of Dent. There are spectacular views on the first half of the ride before returning via Middleton and the Lune valley.

Dent is a traditional village which still has a cobbled main street. There are numerous tea shops and pubs in the village, which provides an interesting place to stop.

Holme Open Farm is directly on the route (tel. 015396 20654). There is no café here, but at the time of publication the entrance fee (£2.00 for adults and £1.50 for children aged three to sixteen) included a cup of coffee/tea and biscuits. There is a conducted farm tour at 2pm, with sheep dogs, pigs, goats and chickens among the things to see. I would advise you phone beforehand, however, if you plan to make a stop here.

There are two pubs on the route – both of which provide bar meals and very traditional atmospheres, making them excellent places to break the journey or relax during the day's ride.

Starting point
The ride starts from the centre of Barbon village, where parking can be found on the road side near the war memorial. To get to Barbon follow signs off the A683 Sedbergh to Kirkby Lonsdale road.

The ride

▷ Head out of Barbon with the war memorial on your right-hand side to pass between the Barbon Inn on your right and the church on your left following signs for Dent. The road goes steeply uphill initially – but don't panic, as this elevation soon eases off.

•Carry straight on past a road off to your right with no signpost.

Cross a cattle grid and another road off to your right signposted 'Casterton and Kirkby Lonsdale'. Continue straight on, signposted 'Dent and Hawes'.

•The road runs alongside a wood on your left-hand side before opening out into Barbondale. You then go alongside Barbon Beck (there are often cars parked here as it provides a good picnic spot) for approximately a mile before pulling

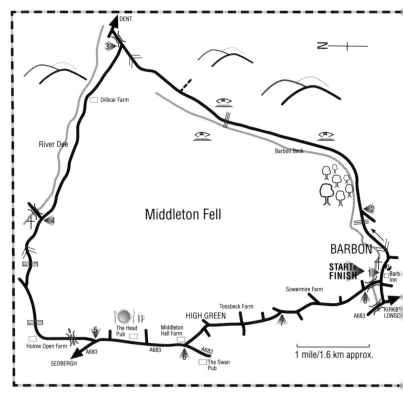

away as the road begins to climb steadily again.

•There are some lovely views here as you work your way up the dale, crossing a cattle grid along the way.

•Once you reach a bridleway off to your right you are nearing the top of the climb and soon begin to descend into the valley of Dentdale, where there are again some fantastic views. The descent is fairly steep at the end so take care.

3▶ At the bottom of the hill you reach a T-junction where you turn left to continue on with the ride – no signpost. If you want to take a short detour of approximately a mile, turn right here to reach the village of Dent.

•Continue along this minor undulating road past several farm buildings and follow it around sharply right past Dillicar Farm.

4▶ Carry along as the road follows the river until you reach a road going off to your right over a bridge. Continue straight on here signposted 'Holme Open Farm' and pass a Methodist chapel on your right.

•The road continues running alongside the river for a short way before veering away to the left and climbing.

•At the top of the hill you come to a gate across the road. Carry along, passing a small road which joins from the right, through the open fields with views of Sedbergh to your right until you reach another gate across the road.

RIDE
13

•Soon after passing this second gate you drop down to reach Holme Open Farm on your right.

5▶ The ride continues along going under an old railway bridge before reaching a T-junction with the main Sedbergh to Kirkby Lonsdale road (A683). Turn left here – there are no signposts.

•You soon pass a small road off to your left, which you ignore. Carry straight on to Middleton and a pub called The Head, which provides bar meals and welcomes children.

•Carry along the main road, passing a small dead-end road off to your left and going under another bridge.

6▶ Take the next small road off to your left next to Middleton Hall Farm. Carry straight along this road, which runs parallel to the main road.

•Pass High Green Farm on your left-hand side and a small road off to your right with a sign 'Unsuitable for Motors'.

Carry straight on down the narrow lane (there are no signposts).

◈ Continue past another small road off to your left, which leads to some farm buildings, and again go straight on at the crossroads at Tossbeck Farm. Carry straight past another small road off to your left and then bear right at the next T-junction (the left turn is a dead end up to some farm buildings).

• Go past Applegarth Farm on your left, and go straight on past a road to your right which leads back to the main road.

◈ Pass yet another small road off to your left, leading to Sowermire Farm, and a dead-end road off to your left, then cross a bridge just before you enter the village of Barbon. At the T-junction in the village you need to turn left to get back to the war memorial and the pub.

FINISH

START

RIDE 14
GRANGE, HOLKER HALL
and CARTMEL PRIORY
TOTAL DISTANCE – 15.5 miles/25.8 km
TERRAIN   – Fairly strenuous

This ride starts in Grange over Sands, a busy little town which boasts a promenade and a beautiful park adjacent to the sea front. There are numerous cafés to relax in, along with a wide variety of shops.

The route takes a minor road past Cartmel Priory. A booklet on this can be obtained from the tourist information centre in Grange, which you pass on your way out of the town. The Priory dates back to the 12th century and is situated in the centre of Cartmel village, itself steeped in history. There are several pubs in the village and numerous tea and gift shops.

The route then climbs steadily up on another minor road before dropping back to the main road to reach Holker Hall and the Lakeland Motor Museum. The museum has over 150 vehicles on display, with an audio visual exhibition featuring the Campbells, who captured 21 world speed records for Great Britain, and including a full size replica of the famous jet hydroplane in which Donald Campbell was killed on Coniston Water in 1967.

Holker Hall dates back to the 16th century and has never been bought or sold, today being a family home to Lord and Lady Cavendish. The house itself is full of pieces of antique furniture and art work, which you can view without the restriction of barriers, and the gardens stretch for some 25 acres. They include many fantastic features and contrasts, and were voted 'amongst the best in the world' by the Good Gardeners' Guide (1997). There is a café, shop and Bird of Prey Centre with displays at 11.30am, 2.00pm and 3.30pm. Leaflets on Holker Hall and the Motor Museum are available from the tourist information office in Grange or from Holker Hall (tel. 015395 58328).

The ride returns back to Grange using minor roads when possible and passing two pubs en route.

Starting point

The starting point of the ride is Grange over Sands.

The ride

▶ Head out of Grange, following signs to 'Cartmel, Holker and Ulverston', along the main street which runs adjacent to the park (the park should be on your left-hand side).

▶ Continue on as the road climbs gently up through the centre of the village to reach a mini-roundabout. At this mini-roundabout bear left, signposted 'Allithwaite, Flookburgh, Cark and Holker Hall'.

• The road then drops down gradually with the sea on your left-hand side. Carry straight on past the Fire Station on your left (the road now becomes Methven Terrace) until you reach a right-hand turn for Cartmel.

▶ Turn right up here into Cartmel Road. This road climbs quite steeply up, passing Middle Fell Gate farm on your left.

• At the top of the hill you reach a crossroads where you go straight across – there is no signpost for straight on. The road now begins to descend fairly steeply as you drop down in to Cartmel village itself. When you reach a T-junction in the village turn right – there are no signposts.

▶ The Pig and Whistle pub is found opposite. Turn immediately left in between the pub and the Spar shop, following a brown sign for Cartmel Priory.

▶ Go along this small road for a short distance before you reach another T-junction. Turn right here. The Priory is now found on your right-hand side and, as mentioned in the introduction to this ride, is an interesting place to stop.

• There are several tea rooms in this area. Follow the road around as it veers sharply left and goes over a small bridge with the Kings Arms pub on your left-hand side. Carry on through the centre of the village, which has lots of interesting tourist shops and Cartmel Priory Gatehouse on your right.

• Continue on as the road bends sharply right in the centre of the village and soon takes you back out to the countryside.

• Pass a road off to your right and continue straight on, sign-posted 'Haverthwaite and Ulverston'. A residential home is found on your right – this was once the old Grammar School.

• You soon pass another road off to your left which is a cul-de-sac. Carry on following signs for Haverthwaite and Ulverston.

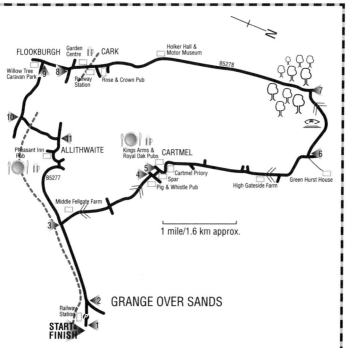

FLOOKBURGH Garden Centre CARK

Holker Hall & Motor Museum

B5278

Willow Tree Caravan Park 9 8

Railway Station Rose & Crown Pub

7

10

11 ALLITHWAITE

Pheasant Inn Pub

Kings Arms & Royal Oak Pubs CARTMEL

B5277

4 5

Cartmel Priory Spar

Pig & Whistle Pub

High Gateside Farm

Green Hurst House

6

Middle Fellgate Farm

3

1 mile/1.6 km approx.

Railway Station

2 GRANGE OVER SANDS

START FINISH 1

RIDE 14

• The road now begins to gradually climb. Ignore the no through road on your left to Speel Bank and continue climbing.

• Pass another small road soon after on your left going

down to some houses, and carry on to pass between the buildings of High Gateside Farm.

•Carry straight on, signposted 'Haverthwaite and Ulverston', past a road off to your right which goes to Lindale and Grange.

6▶ Just before you reach the brow of the hill you need to take a small left-hand turn. There are no signposts here, but the road goes directly under some electric pylons, and the turning is virtually opposite the entrance to a house called Green Hurst House.

•The road immediately begins to descend, with some woods on your left-hand side and some impressive views of the countryside. Continue this descent until you reach a T-junction with the B5278.

7▶ Turn left here – there are no signposts. Carry along, with easy cycling through woods on either side.

•Ignore one small road off to your right and continue on to reach Holker Hall, which is situated on your right-hand side.

• After your break come out of Holker and turn right to continue along the road. Stay on the B5278 through the village of Cark, ignoring all roads off and following signs to Flookburgh and Grange, and passing the Rose and Crown Inn and the railway station both on your left. There is a garden centre with a café on your right-hand side just after the railway station.

8▶ When you reach the village of Flookburgh you come to a 'Give Way' sign. Turn left here and then take a turning immediately to your right signposted to a caravan site. This junction goes around the car park in the village square where there is a signpost.

9▶ There are some public toilets about 50 yards down this road on your right-hand side. Soon after the toilets you pass a small road off to your right which you ignore, taking the next left turning down a single track road. Willow Tree Caravan Park is situated on the corner of this lane.

10▶ You pass through open flat fields on both sides with easy

The River Eden, Appleby-in -Westmorland (Rides 3 and 17)

Beatrix Potter Museum, Hawkshead (Ride 6)

The road following the east shore of Coniston Water (Ride 12)

Cottages in Thwaite Head, Upper Rusland Valley (Ride 8)

cycling, taking the first road off to your left – there are no signposts.

🏵 This road passes over a level crossing before joining back up with the B5277 again at a T-junction. Turn right here, signposted 'Grange'.

• You immediately come to the village of Allithwaite, passing the Pheasant Inn on your right-hand side. This pub provides bar meals and welcomes children.

• Ignore all the roads off to your right and left and continue straight along the B-road into Grange. The road goes gently uphill at first and then levels out before descending once you reach the outskirts of Grange. Carry straight along back to your vehicle, returning via the route you left.

 **FINISH**

RIDE
14

This route runs between the Station Inn pub at Oxenholme and Underley Hall Farm (where there is fruit picking) in Kirkby Lonsdale. You take the quiet minor roads to meander your way to Kirkby, where you can look around the busy market town or pick fruit at Underley Hall. This has an extensive playground for the children as well as picnic tables, and tea, coffee and snacks available. There are toilet facilities but they are very basic, and there are no baby changing facilities.

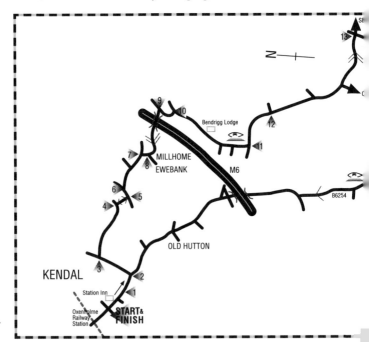

Once you are rested you can begin back along the more direct B6254 to Kendal.

Once under the motorway it's a short way back to the Station Inn pub on the undulating road. The pub has a special room filled with bouncy castles and ball pools called Puffin' Billy's, where you can leave the children supervised for £2.50 an hour whilst you recuperate. Needless to say, there are a children's menu, baby changing facilities, high chairs, and so on in the pub.

Starting point

From Oxenholme railway station, on the outskirts of Kendal, continue uphill for a third of a mile. The Station Inn pub is on the left. Car parking is available here.

The ride

1 Continue along the B6254, signposted 'Old Hutton and Kirkby Lonsdale'.

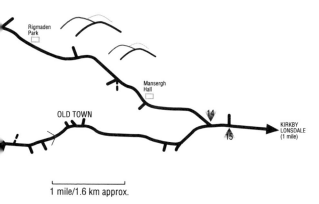

2 Take the first left turn after travelling downhill. There is no signpost, but there is a red letterbox in the wall.

3 Go along this flat minor road and take the first right turn–no signpost.

4 Continue along this undulating road and turn right at the fork – no signpost.

 •Go up a steep, short hill and down another short, steep hill.

5 Turn left at the T-junction – no signpost.

6 In a short distance bear right at the next fork, signposted 'Millholme and Ewebank', and go past the houses of Millholme.

7 Pass one turning to the left and then take the next turning right, signposted 'Ewebank'.

8 At the next T-junction keep left up a steep hill to cross the motorway – do not go into Ewebank. Once past this point most of the hard work for getting to Kirkby is done.

9 Turn right immediately after the motorway (no signpost) and then continue up a very short hill to a T-junction.

10 Turn sharp right (no signpost) and continue on past Bendrigg Lodge (a residential activities holiday centre for disabled children).

11 Continue on, ignoring one road to the right, and carry straight on at the next junction – no signpost. Then take the next left at the T-junction – no signpost to the left, but the right is signposted 'Kendal and Old Hutton'.

12 Continue along and take the first right, signposted 'Old Town and Kirkby Lonsdale'.

 •Pass one road off to the left – no signpost.

 •Continue past a road to your right signposted 'Old Town and Kirkby Lonsdale' and carry straight on, signposted 'Sedbergh'.

Carry on down the steep hill with magnificent views of the Lune valley and take the next right at the crossroads – no signpost.

•Continue along this road for 3¾ miles ignoring any turn-offs. You will pass Rigmaden Park, then Mansergh Hall after 2½ miles, where there is a shop selling free-range pork, handmade sausages and lamb.

Once you have joined the B6254 at the T-junction, turn left into Kirkby Lonsdale and look out for Underley Hall Farm on your left in approximately 50 yards.

Turn left by the signpost for Underley Hall Farm and go over the cattle grid to the farm itself. To visit Kirkby Lonsdale, continue for 1 mile along the B6254, beyond the farm.

•For your return journey, turn right at the road junction on exiting the farm. Head for Kendal following the B6254, signposted 'Kendal and Old Hutton' at any junctions effectively carrying straight on the whole time. This has some gradual ups and downs until Old Town. After this it is a steady pull up to Barkin House on your right.

•Then it's downhill to Old Hutton, and from there just a short ride back to the Station Inn, following the B6254 the whole way to Kendal for a well-earned rest.

FINISH

RIDE 16
DALLAM TOWER to LEIGHTON MOSS NATURE RESERVE

TOTAL DISTANCE – 14 miles/23.3 km
TERRAIN – Moderate

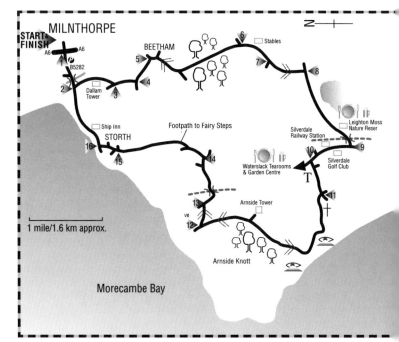

MILNTHORPE

START & FINISH

A6

A6

B5282

BEETHAM

Stables

Dallam Tower

Ship Inn

STORTH

Footpath to Fairy Steps

Silverdale Railway Station

Leighton Moss Nature Reser

Waterslack Tearooms & Garden Centre

Silverdale Golf Club

Arnside Tower

1 mile/1.6 km approx.

Arnside Knot

Morecambe Bay

This route incorporates several places to stop along the way for short walks. These include Leighton Moss Nature Reserve, Arnside Tower, Arnside Knot and the Fairy Steps.

Leighton Moss is run by the RSPB and, along with a selection of walks, has a tea and gift shop, thus providing an interesting place for a break. Arnside Tower is an old stone tower clearly visible from the road, and Arnside Knot is a wooded hill,

70

from the top of which are some excellent views. The Fairy Steps form part of a limestone outcrop approximately 30 feet high through which there is a natural break allowing a scramble to the top which resembles a giant staircase – hence the name.

On the return journey, once all the work has been done, you pass by the Ship Inn, where there is a supply of both liquid and solid refreshments and a fairly large beer garden with a children's play area – this is well situated for a break.

Starting point
The starting point is from the centre of Milnthorpe. Parking can be found close to the traffic lights in the centre of the village in the market square. From the traffic lights follow signs for Crooklands and a heavy goods vehicle testing station. The square can then be found on your right. Market day is on a Friday.

The ride

1. From the traffic lights in the centre of Milnthorpe head out following signs for Arnside (on the B5282).

2. Carry along this road until you cross a bridge. Turn left immediately after the bridge up a small road. This road forms the entrance lane to Dallam Tower, a large stately house.

3. Carry along the lane past Dallam Tower until you reach a T-junction. Turn left at the T-junction – there are no signposts.

4. Continue straight along this road, passing one right-hand turn to Storth and Arnside, and follow signs for Beetham.

5. Drop down into Beetham itself and carry on until you reach the next 'Give Way' at a T-junction. Turn right at this T-junction – there are no signposts. Ignore a road immediately off to your left signposted 'Heron Theatre' and carry straight on, signposted 'Slackhead'.

   • Climb up the steep hill to reach a junction at the summit. You need to carry straight on at this, signposted 'Yealand and Carnforth' (the turning off to your right is signposted 'Silverdale and Arnside').

6▸ Follow the road downhill through woods and past Beetham Caravan Park until you reach your next road junction. Turn right at this junction, signposted 'Arnside, Yealand and Silverdale'.

7▸ Follow the road around, passing a riding stable on your left-hand side. At the next T-junction you need to turn left, signposted 'Yealand Redmayne and Carnforth'. There is a short steep hill which you need to climb, and once you reach the summit you then have a short descent to the next T-junction.

8▸ At this junction you need to turn right, signposted 'Leighton Moss Nature Reserve'. There is another short steep descent before the road flattens out to pass the nature reserve on your left.

• The nature reserve is run by the RSPB. There is a gift shop and a tea room, and several short walks are laid out around the reserve.

9▸ Soon after passing the reserve you reach a T-junction. You need to turn right at this T-junction, which is signposted 'Holgate Camping and Caravanning Park'. You immediately pass Silverdale Golf Club on your left-hand side and Silverdale railway station on your right-hand side.

10▸ Continue on as you pass by some houses and a small dead-end road off to your right. You need to carry on until you reach the next road off to your left, which you take, signposted 'Silverdale'. (If you wish there is a short detour to Waterslack Farm, where there is a garden centre, tea room and gift gallery.)

11▸ Pass a telephone box, bus stop and a small road off to your left called The Row. Carry straight on past Bottoms Lane – a road going off to your left – and immediately take the next right signposted 'Arnside'.

• Go past the church on your left and a small road on your left immediately after the church. Continue straight on along this road, ignoring the roads off to the right and left into the housing estate. Bear right around a sharp bend and continue past Silverdale cricket ground on your left and

Leeds holiday camp and caravan site. The road then drops down to the sea and runs adjacent to it before climbing again and passing another caravaning and camping ground on your left.

•Continue on steadily climbing the hill, passing a small road off to your right which leads down to a farm. (There is a footpath from the farm leading to Arnside Tower, which you can see on the small hill to your right.) There are also footpaths off to your left here leading up to Arnside Knot, where there are excellent views to be had over Morecambe Bay. This is an area of woodland belonging to the National Trust.

The cycle route continues along, climbing for a short distance before dropping down into Arnside itself. As you drop into Arnside and come into the housing estate, ignore the roads off to your right and left which lead into the estate. Continue on descending until you reach a road off to your right signposted 'Yealand and Carnforth'. You need to take this turn (the road is called Brierybank).

Carry along this road as it drops steeply to a T-junction. Turn right here, signposted 'Silverdale and Carnforth'.

The road leads out of Arnside (ignore the small roads going into the housing estate) and goes across the level crossing. Go past Carrbank Road, going off to your left, and take the next left turn, signposted 'Storth'.

•Carry along this road until you reach some farm buildings with a small road off to your left going through the centre of the buildings. Opposite the farm on your right-hand side there is a footpath which leads up to the 'Fairy Steps' (¾ mile away) – a small natural break in a limestone outcrop providing an easy climb which even toddlers can do.

The ride continues along the same road until you reach some crossroads. Go straight across, signposted 'Storth and Sandside'. You soon reach the houses of Storth (carry along ignoring the roads off into the housing estate). Go past the village school on your right-hand side and carry on to reach the next crossroads by a war memorial. Continue straight on through the crossroads.

•Follow the road to the T-junction with the B5282, where you turn right, signposted 'Milnthorpe'.

•The sea is now adjacent to you on your left. You soon reach the Ship Inn on your right-hand side. This has a beer garden, a play area for children and also provides meals. It is a good place to stop before the end of the ride.

•The route continues along to Milnthorpe, passing over the bridge you crossed at the start of the ride before reaching the traffic lights in the centre of Milnthorpe.

•Go straight across the lights to reach your car if you have parked in the market square.

 **FINISH**

START

RIDE 17 APPLEBY CASTLE to WETHERIGG POTTERY

TOTAL DISTANCE – 22 miles/36.6 km
TERRAIN   – Moderate

This is a lovely ride through the roads of Eden, Appleby and Westmorland. The terrain is relatively easy, although the ride may well take most of the day simply because of the distance and the time spent looking around the places of interest en route.

You pass through the villages of Morland and Kings Meaburn, which both have village pubs. The pottery at Wetherigg is well worth a visit, whether cycling or not. Don't forget to leave space in your bag to carry back your works of art (you can throw or paint your own pot). There is also an extensive pottery shop, tea room, playground, museum and some rare breeds of pigs to visit.

This ride can be made shorter by just going between the Pottery and the open farm.

Starting point
Park on the road just opposite the entrance to Appleby Castle.

The ride

RIDE
17

 ▷ Start by cycling uphill past the entrance to Appleby Castle. (Do not cycle into Appleby itself.)
   • Ignore the turning right down Doomgate, which takes you back into the town, and continue along the road.

2▷ Turn right, signposted 'Colby'. Continue out past the hous-es on the outskirts of Appleby, carrying straight on and ignoring turns on the housing estate.

3▷ As you approach Colby and cross the river, follow the road around to the right and continue straight on to the village of Bolton.

•As you enter Bolton, ignore a turning to your left, sign-posted 'Bolton Lodge', and continue straight on through the village, past the school on your left (ignore a turning to your left in the centre of the village signposted 'Kings Meaburn').

4️⃣ Turn left at the crossroads, signposted 'Cliburn, Penrith and Open Farm'.

•Climb gradually uphill before dropping down to the next road junction.

•Continue straight on at this junction, which is signposted to your left 'Open Farm, 1 mile'.

•Ignore a road to your right signposted 'Temple Sowerby and Kirkby Thore' and continue straight on to Cliburn.

•Go past a turning on your right. Cross over the river and continue into the village of Cliburn.

5️⃣ Go straight on at the crossroads in the village. Continue past two turnings to your left and follow signs for 'Penrith'.

•Wetherigg Pottery is found on your left – enjoy your visit!

6️⃣ After a respite, return the way you came, and

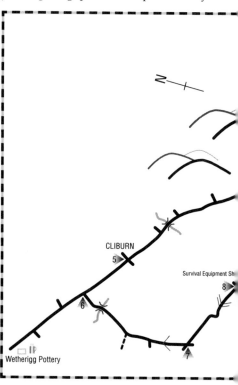

CLIBURN
5️⃣

Survival Equipment Sh
8️⃣

6️⃣

Wetherigg Pottery

take the second right, signposted 'Great Strickland and Newby', about 1 mile before reaching Cliburn.

•Cross a bridge and climb to the top of the hill until you reach the crossroads (ignoring the turning to your right with no signpost).

7▸ Turn left at the crossroads, signposted 'Morland and Appleby'.

8▸ Go straight along this road down a final steep descent into the village of Morland and a T-junction. Turn right here – there is no signpost.

•Ignore the next turning to your right, signposted 'Newby and Shap'. There is a pub in Morland suitable for children –

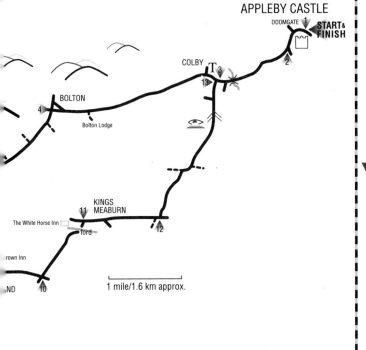

APPLEBY CASTLE

DOOMGATE ▼ START& FINISH

COLBY T 3
13

BOLTON
4

Bolton Lodge

RIDE 17

KINGS
11 MEABURN

The White Horse Inn
ford
12

rown Inn

ND 10

1 mile/1.6 km approx.

the Crown Inn.

• (If you wish to take a diversion to Highgate Farm and Animal Trail, continue straight on, signposted 'Kings Meaburn'. The open farm can be found on your right in less than half a mile.)

If not taking the diversion to the open farm head out of Morland by taking the road to your right. There is no signpost, but the road is opposite Penrith Survival Equipment shop – well worth a look if you're into the outdoors.

Continue along until you reach the crossroads, where you turn left – no signpost to the left.

• Go across Morland moor before descending to the river – cross the ford (always enjoyable for the children) and continue up a short incline to the village of Kings Meaburn, where there is another pub, the White Horse Inn (you need to turn left here to reach that pub).

Turn right through Kings Meaburn, and head out of the village.

• Ignore a right turn to 'Little Beck and Maulds Meaburn' and carry straight on.

Take the next left, signposted 'Colby and Appleby'.

• Continue along this hilly road to reach Colby, ignoring one unsigned turn to your left just before reaching Colby.

Once at the T-junction in Colby itself, turn right and continue back to the castle the way you came.

 **FINISH**

The starting and finishing point of this ride is in the village of Ingleton is a busy market town with an abundance of cafés, pubs and tourist shops, including a pottery. There is a 4 mile waterfall walk which starts near the centre of the village and boasts some impressive cascades. If you do not feel like completing the whole walk it is worth doing the first 1½ miles, since this is where most of the falls are, and there is a little shop selling refreshments to invigorate you for the return journey.

Close to the centre of Ingleton is the first of three impressive viaducts on the route.

This route passes through some classical limestone scenery, taking in Kingsdale, where there are numerous caves, and Twisleton Scar, a limestone outcrop frequently used for climbing.

The ride reaches half way at a welcoming pub, the Sportmans Inn, which provides bar meals in a pleasant surrounding, before climbing up Dent Head to pass under the viaduct carrying the Settle to Carlisle railway line. Once you join the main Hawes to Ingleton road the terrain becomes easier as you pass amongst impressive scenery before passing the Ribblehead Viaduct – an imposing bit of architecture.

You return to Ingleton by a minor road which runs alongside Twisleton Scar. The scenery here is so idyllic it is often featured in films.

Starting point
The starting point is in Ingleton village itself. There is a large car park in the centre of this busy market village which is convenient to use and has public toilets adjacent.

The ride

▷ From the main car park in the centre of the village follow signs for 'Thornton-in-Lonsdale' and brown signs for the waterfall walk. This will take you down a steep hill and over two bridges.

2 Continue past the car park heading out of Ingleton, going under the viaduct and past Holme Head caravan park on your left.

3 Turn right at the first junction you come to, signposted 'Thornton-in-Lonsdale, Dent and St Oswalds church'.

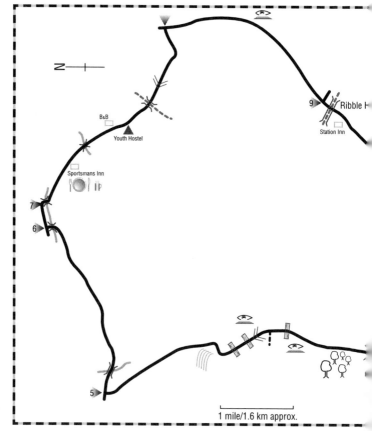

•Carry along until you reach the church on your right and a pub, the Marton Arms, which serves excellent bar meals and has a total of 15 different real ales to sample.

4▶ Take the right-hand turn opposite the pub, signposted 'Dent'.

•This road climbs quite steeply up. Once you pass a road off to your left to Westhouse you have nearly reached the top.

•Carry straight on, signposted 'Dent', with brilliant views of limestone pavements to your left. The road then drops

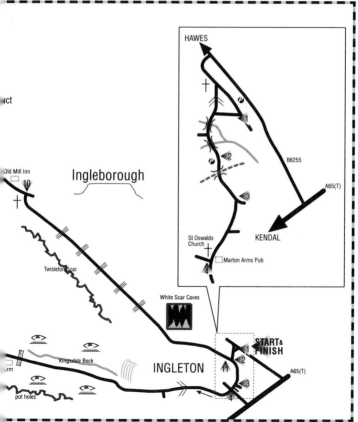

down to join Kingsdale Beck. On your descent, if you look to your right-hand side you can often see an ice cream van parked on the bridleway (to take advantage of people on the waterfall walk). This can be easily reached from a lay-by adjacent to the bridleway.

• The road now travels along the valley of Kingsdale with its stunning scenery. Carry along the road, passing Kingsdale Head Farm, where there is a gate across the road.

• The road ascends very steeply at first past some woods on the left, and then eases off a little to pass through another gate across the road with some fantastic views of the valley panning out behind.

• As you reach the top of the climb and begin to descend you pass a bridleway on your left, where you now have views over into Dentdale and beyond. The road now descends **very** steeply down into Deepdale. There are two gates to pass through on your descent – so beware.

• Once through the second gate the descent soon eases off. Look out for an impressive waterfall on your left-hand side next to the road.

5 Carry along this road as it gradually descends into Dentdale, passing several farm buildings on the way, until you reach a triangular junction. Turn right here, signposted 'Dent Head'.

• The road at first descends and then becomes undulating as you gradually work your way up the valley past one small dead-end road off to your right. Carry along until you eventually come to a T-junction immediately after crossing a small bridge.

6 Turn right here – there are no signposts. Go past St John the Evangelist church on your left-hand side and cross a bridge before coming into the village of Cowgill.

7 Ignore a road off to your left signposted to 'Dent station and Garsdale Head' and carry along, following the road around to the right and crossing over another bridge before swinging left again to run alongside the river.

• You soon reach a pub, the Sportmans Inn, which provides

bar meals and a comfortable place to break the journey.

•Follow the road along as it goes across another bridge and past Scow Cottage bed and breakfast on your left and the Youth Hostel on your right.

•The road now begins to climb steeply up, passing under a viaduct carrying the Settle to Carlisle railway line. This is the last big pull of the ride.

8▶ The road then plateaus out before joining the main Hawes to Ingleton road at a T-junction. Turn right at this junction, signposted 'Ingleton and Settle'.

•Carry along this road, with easy cycling and good views of Ingleborough in front of you and of the impressive Ribblehead Viaduct.

9▶ As you near the viaduct you pass a road off to your left signposted 'Horton in Ribblesdale'. Carry straight on, signposted 'Ingleton and White Scar Caves'. There is often a snack van parked at this junction.

•You cross a cattle grid immediately before a pub, the Station Inn, on your right-hand side which provides bar meals.

10▶ The road now begins to gradually descend with Ingleborough on your left-hand side. Go past another pub, Old Hill Inn, on your left-hand side. Once past the pub you need to look out for a road off to your right signposted 'Chapel-le-dale church'. Take this turning and continue on past the church.

•The road crosses a total of five cattle grids whilst it runs alongside Twisleton Scar – a popular place for climbers.

•You can clearly see White Scar Caves on the other side of the valley. As you pass a quarry on your left the road begins to descend into the village of Ingleton.

11▶ Once you reach the T-junction at the bottom of the hill you turn left to take you back to the car park.

START

RIDE 19 HIGH NEWTON to FELL FOOT COUNTRY PARK

TOTAL DISTANCE – 11.5 miles/19.2 km
TERRAIN – Strenuous

This is a fairly strenuous ride, starting with the gradual ascent of Newton Fell. The height gained is rewarded with fantastic views out over the Kent estuary and Whitbarrow Scar before descending into Bowland Bridge.

There then follows a long uphill section passing the Masons Arms, which serves real ales and bar meals. Your efforts are made worthwhile with extensive views of Lake Windermere after you pass the summit of this climb. The long descent takes you down to Fell Foot Country Park, on the shores of Lake Windermere.

Alternatively, you could break the journey at a Forestry Commission picnic ground called Gummer's How, which can be found on your left at the start of the descent.

The facilities at Fell Foot include a tea room and shop, rowing boat hire, access to the lake shore, a picnic area and an adventure playground. The park is owned by the National Trust. The tea rooms are open from 11am to 5pm daily. The ride returns via quiet tree-lined back lanes, returning you to the start point

Starting point

Starting point is in High Newton. If approaching on the A590 trunk road from Kendal to Newby Bridge, turn into High Newton on your right. A little park can be found opposite the Duck and Crown Inn. There is plenty of parking to be found along the roadside next to the park and village hall. If approaching from Barrow, turn left off into High Newton from the A590 trunk road.

The ride

1▸ Head out of High Newton on the road signposted 'Cartmel

Fell', with the Duck and Crown Inn on your right.

Carry on up the short hill to a fork in the road signposted 'Witherslack' to the right and no signpost to the left. Take

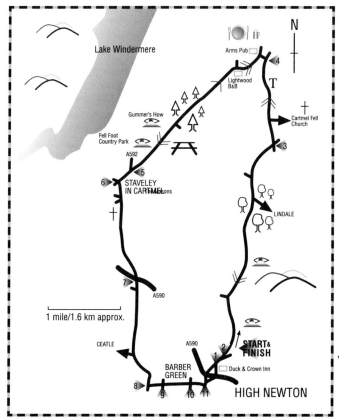

Lake Windermere

Arms Pub

N

Lightwood
B&B

T

Gummer's How

Cartmel Fell
Church

Fell Foot
Country Park

A592

3

5

6

STAVELEY
IN CARTMEL

LINDALE

7

A590

1 mile/1.6 km approx.

CEATLE

A590

2

START &
FINISH

BARBER
GREEN

Duck & Crown Inn

8

9

10

11

HIGH NEWTON

RIDE
19

the left fork with no signpost. The road flattens out and there are good views of Morecambe Bay on the right-hand side. Carry on past a road to your left with no signpost and the farm entrance.

•Continue down the long descent until you reach the next road junction, in the middle of a wood with a road off to your right signposted 'Lindale'. Do not take this road but carry straight on. Also ignore the next turning to your left with no signpost.

3▶ Continue along to the crossroads, where you turn left, signposted 'Church and Bowness'. Go straight on past a road on your right signposted 'Cartmel Fell Church'. There is no signpost for the straight road.

4▶ Continue down a steep hill and pass a telephone box on your right. Carry on to a T-junction and turn left, signposted 'Newby and Ulverston'. You will find yourself at the bottom of a steep hill, which you can always walk up. Just at the beginning of the ascent there is a road off to the right, and a pub called the Masons Arms – in case you need some sustenance to get you up the hill! This pub also does meals.

• Continue straight on up the hill past the Lightwood bed & breakfast farmhouse on your left, ignoring the road off to your right, which is just opposite. Once you have passed a forestry road off to your right, and one immediately off to your left, you are nearing the top of the hill.

• Continue on as the road becomes gradually more gentle. Go straight past a turning to the left and continue up the last bit of hill. As you begin to go down, look out for fantastic views of Lake Windermere on your right. Just at the beginning of the descent on the left-hand side there is a parking area with picnic tables – a very good place to stop for a rest and some food.

5▶ Next is a long descent of nearly a mile down to a T-junction and the main A592 road. At the T-junction turn right to Fell Foot Country Park, which is about 100 yards on your left.

6▶ Once you've visited Fell Foot Country Park, return to the A592 road. Turn right onto the main road and immediately take the first left, signposted 'Staveley in Cartmel'.

• As you are going through the village of Staveley, ignore a turning to your right (there are no signposts here) and carry straight on past a telephone box on your left.

• Ignore the next turning off to your right and carry straight on, signposted 'Church, Grange and Lancaster'.

▷ Go past the church on your right-hand side. Once you have reached the A590, you need to go straight across, signposted 'Cartmel and Priory'. Take care crossing, as this is a notoriously busy road.

•Go past a turning on your right soon after the junction and follow the straight road, ignoring another turning right which is signposted 'Ceatle'.

▷ Take the next turning left, which is not signposted.

▷ Continue straight on at the next crossroads, signposted 'Barber Green', and go straight through this village.

▷ Just as you exit you come across another crossroads, which is not signposted, as you begin to climb the hill. Go straight on.

▷ Once you reach the T-junction at the top of the hill, turn left. There are no signposts into the centre of High Newton. Go straight down through the village to join the A590, which you cross to bring you to the other side of High Newton, signposted 'Cartmel Fell', and your vehicle.

 **FINISH**

RIDE
19

The starting point of the ride is in a car park near the head of the idyllic Duddon valley, where there are short forest walks, picnic tables and a river running adjacent to the car park. It makes an ideal place to both start and relax at the end of the ride.

The ride itself starts by gradually gaining height to the base of Hardknott Pass. Once traversed, there then follows a long descent to Eskdale before returning via Barker Fell and the Duddon valley. This is a ride which takes you right into the heart of the Lakes with very impressive scenery en route.

The Ravenglass to Eskdale railway provides an ideal spot to break your journey. This is England's oldest narrow gauge railway, opened in 1875, and runs for some 7 miles (tel. 01229 717171 to check the timetable for the trains). If you choose to go all the way to Ravenglass you can visit the railway museum and a pub called the Ratty Arms which provides bar meals. Or you can break the journey at Muncaster water mill, where you can see flour being milled in the traditional way.

The return journey from Ravenglass takes approximately two hours, so you do need to allow plenty of time. There is a café at Dalegarth station, where you break your journey, which serves a vast range of food and the inevitable ice creams. Picnic tables are provided adjacent to the car park next to the station, with Whillan Beck, a small river, running through to add to the tranquillity.

arting point

rking is at Birks Bridge Forestry Enterprise car park, between the
llage of Seathwaite in the Duddon valley and the head of the valley
elf. If approaching from Ambleside head for Little Langdale and
oss over Wrynose Pass to reach the base of Hardknott Pass, where
u turn left and head down the Duddon valley for nearly 2 miles to
d the car park on your right-hand side. If approaching from the

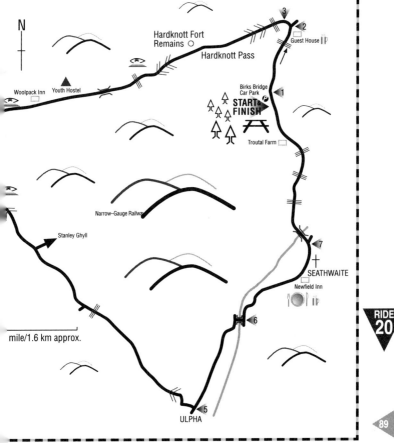

N

Hardknott Fort
Remains ○

Hardknott Pass

Birks Bridge
Car Park

Woolpack Inn   Youth Hostel

START
FINISH

1

2

3

Guest House

Troutal Farm

Narrow-Gauge Railway

Stanley Ghyll

7

SEATHWAITE

Newfield Inn

mile/1.6 km approx.

6

5

ULPHA

RIDE
20

89

south travel up the Duddon valley from Duddon Bridge past Seathwaite until you reach the car park on your left-hand side.

The ride

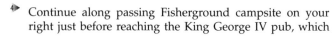

1. Turn left out of the car park entrance and carry along, crossing over a cattle grid.

2. Turn left immediately after the cattle grid, signposted 'Eskdale via Hardknott Pass'. There is a guest house at this junction which sells tea, coffee and ice cream.

3. Cross the bridge and the cattle grid to begin the ascent of Hardknott Pass. The climb is fairly gradual initially but does get very steep towards the end, where the hairpin bends are. It does not take long to walk up this bit of the pass, which you will probably find you need to do.

   • There are spectacular views of the Duddon valley and Eskdale on your descent. The descent is not quite as steep as the ascent, although you do need to take great care.

   • Just after the steepest bit of the descent you pass Hardknott Fort – an old Roman fort which is easily accessible from the roadside on your right.

   • Continue the descent, crossing a cattle grid, after which the road levels out.

   • You cross a bridge and pass the Youth Hostel on your right-hand side before reaching the Woolpack Inn, where bar meals are provided against a backdrop of outstanding Lakeland scenery.

   • Continue along to pass a dead-end right-hand turn to Boot and Brookhouse Inn and Restaurant. Soon after passing these you reach Eskdale railway on your right-hand side – as mentioned in the introduction to the ride, this is an ideal spot to break the journey.

   • Once rested exit the car park and turn right to continue on down the road.

   • Pass a small road off to your left and cross a bridge with the railway line now immediately on your right-hand side.

4. Continue along passing Fisherground campsite on your right just before reaching the King George IV pub, which

serves bar meals. At the T-junction next to the pub you need to turn left, signposted 'Ulpha and Broughton'.

• Carry along, crossing a bridge and passing a small road off to your right signposted 'Birkby Road'. Continue straight on, signposted 'Ulpha and Broughton'.

• The road begins to ascend up Birker Fell. You cross a cattle grid before the road begins to climb steeply. Don't forget you can always get off and walk.

• Impressive views of the Lakeland mountain scenery can be seen as you near the summit. Once you reach a small road off to your left signposted 'Stanley Ghyll', you have done the worst of the climbing. Carry straight on, signposted 'Ulpha and Broughton'.

• After a further short, easy incline you can enjoy a long descent into Ulpha, passing a small road off to your right which leads to farm buildings and crossing a cattle grid en route.

• Just before you reach the village of Ulpha and the T-junction the road descends **steeply** around some hairpin bends.

5 At the T-junction you need to turn left, signposted 'Seathwaite and Langdale via Wrynose Pass'.

• Carry along this road as it heads up the Duddon valley, with the river Duddon on your right-hand side initially, and then cross a bridge, where there is a small dead-end road off to your left.

6 Pass a turning to your right, signposted 'Broughton Mills', immediately after the bridge and carry straight on, signposted 'Seathwaite and Wrynose'. The river Duddon is now on your left-hand side.

• Continue until you reach the village of Seathwaite, where a pub, the Newfield Inn, can be found on your right-hand side in the centre of the village. This provides bar meals, and is a popular place for walkers to stop.

• Carry on through the village, passing the church on your right-hand side. The road now begins to climb steadily, and is tree lined on either side with the river running close by on your left-hand side.

When you reach a fork in the road you need to bear left, signposted 'Langdales via Wrynose'.

• You cross a bridge and go up a short, steep ascent before the road elevation eases off again.

• Go across a total of three cattle grids and pass Troutal Farm on your left-hand side before reaching the car park at Birks Bridge on your left-hand side.

FINISH

START

RIDE 21 CROSTHWAITE, UNDER-BARROW and CROOK
TOTAL DISTANCE – 12.5 miles/20.8 km
TERRAIN – Fairly strenuous

This ride passes by a total of five pubs or hotels, all providing meals and drinks to the weary cyclist. The pubs are all essentially village inns with traditional décor.

The Gilpin Lodge Hotel is a four-star hotel which provides morning coffee, luncheon and afternoon teas. The Wild Boar Hotel is a three-star hotel also serving lunch and bar meals.

There is also an excellent playground en route which makes a very good place to stop for a picnic if you do not want to take advantage of the local amenities.

Although fairly short, the ride involves several **hard** climbs. It is almost entirely on quiet country lanes with impressive views of the surrounding Lakeland fells.

Starting point
There are two lay-bys on the B5284 Bowness on Windermere to Kendal road between the Gilpin Lodge Country House Hotel and the Wild Boar Hotel. Either of these lay-bys can be used for parking.

The ride

1. From your lay-by head out towards Crook and Kendal along the B2584. Take the first turning on your right, directly opposite the Wild Boar Hotel. This is a small road going very steeply downhill initially.

2. You quickly come across a junction where you turn right – no signpost.
   - Carry along this road as it goes gently downhill past Mitchlland Farm bungalow (a disabled bed and breakfast) on your right.

3. The road then climbs before reaching the next junction, where there is a road going off to the left. There are no signposts, but you need to take this left turn.
   - Follow this road as it descends steeply down and bears sharply around to the left, with a sign to Crosthwaite and Bateman Fold.
   - Carry on descending until you cross a small bridge at the bottom of the hill, and then go up a short incline to reach a T-junction.

4. Turn right here, signposted 'Crosthwaite'. The road now begins to descend. Follow the road along as you pass several farms and houses until you reach your next junction. Carry straight on at this junction, signposted 'Crosthwaite'.

5. You are now on the outskirts of Crosthwaite village itself, and you need to turn left at the next T-junction, signposted 'Kendal' (this is the main road through the village of Crosthwaite).
   - Carry straight on through the village, passing the post office on your left-hand side and then the playground on your right just before the school, also on your right. This is an excellent place to stop with young children.
   - The Punch Bowl can be found on your right-hand side past the school.
   - Once out of the village of Crosthwaite you need to carry

RIDE
21

straight on, ignoring a turning to your right signposted 'Lancaster', a turning off to your left with no signpost, and another turning off to your left signposted 'Redscar and Broom Farm'.

6️⃣ Once you pass the sign for Underbarrow itself, there is a small road off to your right signposted 'Milnthorpe and Levens'. Ignore this right turn and carry straight on, signposted 'Staveley and Kendal'.

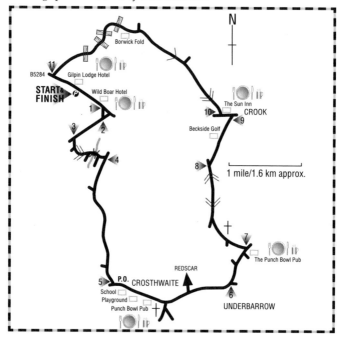

• You quickly come across another road off to your left, signposted 'Crook and Staveley'. Ignore this turning and carry straight on to reach the Punch Bowl pub at Underbarrow. This provides real ale and bar meals in a traditional setting.

7️⃣ The pub is situated on your right, just by a road junction. Ignore the road off to your right, signposted 'Brigsteer', and take the left turn, signposted 'Crook', directly opposite the pub.

•Continue straight along this road, ignoring a road off to your left signposted 'Crosthwaite'.

•Pass All Saints church on your right before beginning to climb. Ignore a turning to the left with no signpost at the beginning of the hill.

8▶ After your climb the road then descends before reaching another turning off to your left, again with no signpost, which you ignore.

9▶ After a short distance you reach a T-junction in the centre of Crook. Turn left here, signposted 'Bowness and Windermere golf course'.

10▶ Go past the Sun Inn and take the next turn on your right – no signpost.

•This road climbs steeply uphill before descending and then flattening out.

•Go straight past a very small road off to your right, signposted 'Dalesway', and climb a further hill before reaching the next road off to your right with a cattle grid. There are no signposts here, but you need to continue straight on.

•The road passes Borwick Fold, a farmhouse, before reaching a gate across the road. Go straight through this gate and the next gate at the other end of the field.

11▶ You pass through some picturesque countryside before descending down to reach the T-junction with the B5284. Turn left at this T-junction – there are no signposts.

•You will soon pass the Gilpin Lodge Hotel on your left-hand side, where you can stop or continue on to the lay-by and your car.

RIDE
21

FINISH

OTHER CYCLE GUIDES BY CICERONE

THE CHESHIRE CYCLE WAY *Alec & Val Scaresbrook* 135 mile circular ride around rural Cheshire, described in 18 easy stages. *ISBN 1 85284 204 0 96pp*

THE CUMBRIA CYCLE WAY *Roy Walker & Ron Jarvis* 212 miles around Cumbria with 21 maps, and details of local geology, history and landscape. *ISBN 1 85284 106 0 128pp*

LANDS END TO JOHN O'GROATS CYCLE GUIDE *Simon Brown* A 14 day ride through Britain from south to north. Includes accommodation, planning, maintenance and everything the cyclist is likely to want to know. *ISBN 1 85284 188 5 116pp*

THE LLEYN PENINSULA COASTAL PATH *John Cantrell* Starting at Caernarfon the coastal path goes round the peninsula to Porthmadog following the old Bardsey Pilgrims' route. Described for walkers and cyclists. *ISBN 1 85284 252 0 168pp*

ON THE RUFFSTUFF 84 bike rides in northern England *J.Brian Beadle* From reservoir tracks and old railways, moorland paths and parkland, canal towpaths and the Trans-Pennine Trail. This book has something for everyone. *ISBN 1 85284 190 7 184pp*

RURAL RIDES No1 WEST SURREY *Ron Strutt* Family rides graded from easy to more challenging, between Farnham and Leatherhead. *ISBN 1 85284 272 5 160pp*

RURAL RIDES No2 EAST SURREY *Ron Strutt* Family rides between Dorking and Lingfield. *ISBN 1 85284 273 3 160pp*

THE SCOTTISH GLENS Books 1-9 *P.D. Koch-Osborne* See detailed list under SCOTLAND

THE WAY OF ST JAMES - A Cyclist's Guide *John Higginson* A guide for touring cyclists to follow the ancient pilgrimage route of the Way of St James from Le Puy to Santiago. *ISBN 1 85284 274 1 108pp*

EXPLORE THE WORLD WITH A CICERONE GUIDE

Cicerone publishes over 280 guides for walking, trekking, climbing and exploring the UK, Europe and worldwide. Cicerone guides are available from outdoor shops, quality book stores and from the publisher.

Cicerone can be contacted on
www.cicerone.co.uk
www.ciceroneguides.com